ALSO BY JONATHAN ALDRICH

Books

Croquet Lover at the Dinner Table 1977
Wade's Wait 1985
The Death of Michelangelo 1985
The Ring Road 2007
The Storks of Edam 2010
Foam: A Poetic Sequence 2012
Injury 2013
Out of St. Orange 2015

Chapbooks

Le Voyage, a translation (with drawings by Alison Hildreth) 1998
Figures 2000
Sonnets for Grimm 2000
Family Romance (with etchings by Alison Hildreth) 2009

THE OLD WORLD IN HIS ARMS

THE OLD WORLD IN HIS ARMS
Collected Poems

by
Jonathan
Aldrich

Wolfson Press
South Bend
2021

Grateful acknowledgment is made
to editors of publications where
some of these poems first appeared.
They are listed at the end of this volume.

Cover design by Sky Santiago.
Cover Painting, *Solo at Dusk*, by Ed Douglas.
Interior design by Sky Santiago, Michael Kouroubetes
and Kurt Lott.

Copyright © 2021 by Nancy Aldrich
All rights reserved. First edition.

ISBN: 978-1-950066-10-0

Wolfson Press
Master of Liberal Studies Program
Indiana University South Bend
1700 Mishawaka Avenue
South Bend, Indiana 46615
WolfsonPress.com

CONTENTS

CROQUET LOVER AT THE DINNER TABLE
5	Bread
6	Winter Fantasy
7	A Shaker Girl (c. 1850)
12	Fruitlands, 1950
13	Homage to Shakers
14	The Glassblower
15	To a Young Lady at the Museum
16	Croquet Lover at the Dinner Table
17	Passion of Crows
18	Suite
19	Country Matters
20	Before the Prophet
21	Watchers
22	Van Gogh: *Starry Night*
23	Loss of the Unicorn
24	Bells
25	November
26	Tiger Lilies
27	At Home
28	Willow Street
29	Traveling West

WADE'S WAIT
35	Lustings
51	Dinner Was Served
75	Pool Shot
103	The Shade Trees

THE RING ROAD
I
119	*Before my brother was born*
119	*In summer the fireflies*
120	*So many gods pour out*
120	*The goblins underneath*
121	*White snow against the red*
121	*Music is still a mystery*

122	*If a holiday turkey is sliced*
122	*Her toe on the carpet. A buzz,*
123	*Leaving his family, a child*
123	*They said a stranger hid*
124	*The world is off, and we*
124	*I say a dream is like*
125	*Although his talk was always*
125	*Blizzard. . . . Mount Auburn Street*

II

126	*The young fall in love instantly,*
126	*Letting her underthings*
127	*First only a few feathers*
127	*I feel them both—a warm*
128	*I wish I could find an answer*
128	*Better to wear your sword*
129	*Nor are the 59*
129	*The piano she has moved*
130	*Some have taken the lapse*
130	*Say you're meandering*
131	*When a kaleidoscope*
131	*The underground is good.*

III

132	*I can hardly see you*
132	*These are the warm shadows*
133	*Rubbing my eyes and nearly*
133	*"Oh, no, the intellectual*
134	*Like a mobile over*
134	*My daughter felt that poison*
135	*Mrs. Christie hopes we'll*
135	*In praise of folly?—yes,*
136	*The double-chalice of*
136	*God of unknown, of days*
137	*Now the mirror only*
137	*Still there is only one*

IV

138	*Our neighborhood is changing*
138	*The Burren is a great*
139	*Mairena offers no bar*
139	*The long river of Prague*
140	*In the low-lit chapel*

140	*It makes me think how long*
141	*In England where we chose*
	V
142	*It may boil down to your hat,*
142	*So here's the interior's*
143	*We came to another signpost*
143	*The sea being inside*
144	*Idly she doodles right*
144	*Did no Great Spirit come*
145	*She found there was nothing quite*
145	*Beacon Hill: good food*
146	*You can't go home again?*
146	*My graying head I find*
147	*My father under the Gainsborough*
147	*When there is very little*
148	*Where the Unconscious seems*
148	*The first people stay alive*
149	*What we have thrown away,*
149	*At night return the place-names*
150	*A rain begins to fall*

THE DEATH OF MICHELANGELO

153	Introduction
155	To Vittoria Colonna
156	In the Sistine Chapel
157	For Dante
158	On Creation
159	To Tomasso
160	To His Father
161	On Aging
162	On His Conversion
163	The Rondanini

SONNETS FOR GRIMM

167	Blue Shoes
168	A Riddle
169	The Wicked Healer
170	Even the Wizard Wondering
171	The Cruel Mother
172	Homeward

173	Brother in the Well
174	The Mirror
175	Ashputtle
176	The Swans

FLACKER IN PARIS
177

FOAM
197	Study
197	Gama and Gampa
198	The Tale of the Dinghy
205	Harts Neck Road
205	Rich
206	The Sway of the Sea
206	Family Cruise
207	Hymn-Sing
207	Gone Now
208	My Favorite Deep-Voiced Neighbor
208	The Gift
209	Burial at Sea
210	Heron at Morning
211	Night: the Water Bearer
211	Song to N.

TIVOLI
215	Song One: Get Out of Town
222	Song Two: How Little We Know
230	Song Three: Cool Water
238	Song Four: These Foolish Things
246	Song Five: Honeysuckle Rose ...

OWED TO *FINNEGANS WAKE*
253

GENERATION
275

NEW AND SELECTED
| 301 | Christmas Letter |
| 302 | The Carriage Man |

303	Our Westie, Robert
304	The Bird of Paradise
306	The Constellations Are Not Fixed
307	Soldier Poet
308	The Blot
312	The Mother
313	Child Poet
316	All Poets Love Thunderstorms
317	My Father's Prophecy (1914)
318	Of Unknowing
319	Ars Poetica
320	On Form
321	Belief
322	Whitestone Pond
323	Mexican Arabesque
324	Wedding Poem for Megan and Peter
325	The Storks of Edam
326	Places in Mind
328	Nervous
329	Styx
330	Ideas as Things
331	Undressing the Salad
332	The Field
333	After Long Illness
334	R.I.P.
335	The Father
336	How Joe Got Zen
341	Trolls
342	Prospero Young and Old
344	We Think of Arthur / Toní / Duane
345	Solstice
346	Jumping

ACKNOWLEDGMENTS

Dedicated to
Phyllis and (the memory of) Jerry Hughes

THE OLD WORLD IN HIS ARMS

Late late yestreen I saw the new moone,
Wi the auld moone in her arme,
And I feir, I feir, my deir master,
That we will cum to harme.
 —*from "Sir Patrick Spens," anonymous Scottish ballad*

Savage is he who saves himself.
 —*Leonardo da Vinci*

from
CROQUET LOVER AT THE DINNER TABLE

*how many morning glories
have walked down to the sea
filling their blue nets?*

BREAD

There are many ways to live. Whole wheat
is tasty, so are rye and white

and sesame, oatmeal, acorn, maize,
bread tanning forever on trays

of dawn—in factories
and towns, on farms at first light,

even the settled hermit waking
breaks it again, this common thing.

As for me, I'd say one loaf
a day could be enough:

bread for your morning visit, bread
and honey, or bread with tea and marmalade.

Let nobody go wanting, and let the grain
be fresh and broken by the moving sun.

WINTER FANTASY

This for my-lady's neckpiece:—
they have let the red fox go,
and the bell on his collar
tinkles out of the morning, over the snow.

Picture five hunters riding
brown horses with black tails who, at a horn,
turn from the center of the morning
into the yellow sun

(one hunter remembering hills of the home
he cursed), the low hounds nosing ahead
where the fox has clipped the bright crust, his track
a skitter of beads;

and a faraway sled
glides down a hill, its trail
curved like an elephant's tusk (one hunter remembers the curl

of his dead child) as they pass through a dwindling brake
—its gray twigs turned like spokes of an ignited wheel—
to an etched hollow, and hard lake, maintaining
a simple tree, with limbs fringe-white
above and black below, suitable for hanging,
as the pack, all prinked and singing,
swerves to a call.

Fur bristling,
their quarry holds at a bush,
compact, his collar bell
still tinkling, trying with a paw
to shake it off—too late!—
They are leaping the last hedge, crying—
as he goes, in a flash, abstract,
his eyes blown white.

A SHAKER GIRL (c.1850)

i. The Snake

Craftily it spoke
and, as everything fell
into place, was seen
(they say) to disappear,
subtle and quick,
behind the evergreen,
its blood-berry and song,
and there to coil
like a sundial—

making us wrong
simply in being here?

ii. The Millennial Laws

From chaos, first, came word
of time; and out of the jaws
of time came our good Lord
and the Millennial Laws.

He is our very cause.
And while, with the others here,
I shake and dance—it is
"contrary to order" for

Believers to rest the feet
on the rounds of chairs,
or, ascending, to put
the left foot first on stairs;

to offer the world greeting;
to have right and left shoes;
or, when going to meeting,
not to walk on toes.

To nickname; to mix any
seed with another seed;
to keep a beast for fancy,
or lie curled in bed.

Or own watches; in the halls
to go blinking or yawning;
to tell nonsensical tales.
And is there no returning?

iii. Half-Song

Lord, protect our tender grapes,
and watch the Bible on my shelf;
note my charity and hopes.

The tiger lilies, burning gaps
along the wall, wait like a wolf—
Lord, protect the tender grapes.

Hands are nothing more than cups
to catch the sunlight for itself:
note my charity and hopes.

As I wander by the crops
I feel a frightening, small gulf.
(Lord, protect the tender grapes.)

Unplanted, I repeat in loops:
the seed is split and views itself.
Note my charity and hopes.

Can this be loneliness? Perhaps.
It is, if only I myself
(O Lord) protect the tender grapes,
note my charity and hopes.

iv. Walking Home

Just yesterday, in passing by the water,
we saw a spotted snake, its life in order,
slipping between the reeds, out of our way,
and screamed: to see how surely a snake works
on our very brookside, how its scales are dark
and shiny, and each eye a tiny world.

I have walked here alone. It makes a world
of difference to sit down and build a water-
wheel of some twigs and branches, in the dark
of the old stone bridge—sitting alone in order
that no one can know the wheel is here and works
by itself at night, under the Milky Way.

We like to think ours is the only way,
this formal separation from the world.
We pray, and shake, and learn to do good works,
and I pick herbs and berries, bake, and water
the animals—but like the fruits I order
in boxes, do I lie changing in the dark?

Little by little, I see myself as dark,
intelligent and pretty, measured that way,
too "contumacious" for the Children's Order
that tucks me in—oh, such a tidy world.
Seeing the April blossoms, my eyes water
just for the sake of anything that works.

Nobody shakes and dances, prays or works
harder than I myself, although at dark
I lie awake and wonder: if Holy water
won't take on me, perhaps the "primrose way,"
whatever that can be, for all the world,
is merrier than these winters we keep by order.

Someday let's take off shoes and stockings, order
our frocks by the willow where the brook works
with light unbraided currents into the world.
We'll keep our village elders in the dark
if suddenly our temperate wills give way
to floating palm-leaf bonnets over water:

White boats in racing order, each a world
of violet and dark fern, our handiwork
may carry wayside flowers to bright water.

FRUITLANDS, 1950

> Blankets and Comfortables should be of a modest color, not checked, striped, or flowered.... One rocking chair in a room is sufficient.... Believers should not keep any beast that needs an extravagant portion of whipping or beating, but such had better be sold to the children of this world, or killed....
> —from the Millennial Laws, 1821

"So when a Shaker died," our guide
explains, "they put him in a pine
unpainted coffin, sometimes with
only initials, age and date
on a small marker facing west,
in simple rows...."
                A room brightened
as if by skylight—somehow a faint
pinwheel attraction floating over
us. And how to move in this?
No people left, no animal
or mouse, nothing alive at all!
And if they never wanted babies,
why that little cradle there?
How long since the last gathering
in song and dance we hear about,
meetings when a whole community
went shaking into the small hours?
Many questions I don't ask.
The light swallows jangle outside
to the day's undoing, as we go round
and round the inventions of an old
order—a circular saw, the first
flat brooms and metal pens, a palm-
leaf bonnet loom, and common clothespin,
left to the children of this world.

HOMAGE TO SHAKERS

Now a traveler sees
   the local show
of chairs and recipes
   you kept, and how

sweetly a song runs through
   these fragrant ponds
and orchards, where you knew
   the first bonds.

Only an owl (the sly
   neighbor) keeps
an elm comfortably
   tonight: he sleeps

apart, in branches near
   your chosen graveyard,
or wakes to an austere
   silence—tired

and curious sentinel,
   but like a cross,
working to dispel
   an old loss.

One may envy
   that beautifully false
neutrality;
   but when she calls,

a nesting whippoorwill
   allows that it
was only natural,
   your dying out.

THE GLASSBLOWER

His, too, is a clear study
against the least crystal
or seed, keeping the stress and fragrance
of a blackbird floating in the rain
like a prime number,
or a Mondrian,

or a clove—its small
and formal kindling on the tongue.
He works in winter, loving
children not his own

who, at the fair,
will see his orange liquor pale
and snake to an amazed bubble to conjure
a vase, a flower,

    and take from there
a sudden little ecstasy, a fear.

TO A YOUNG LADY AT THE MUSEUM

Considering life, for once, in terms of art
I remember what a teacher said to me
(quoting Aristotle, I believe)
that the possible improbability
is less acceptable, in art, than the
probable impossibility.

That is to say: babies have been known
to tumble seven stories to the ground
without sustaining any injury
beyond a minor shakedown.
Just the other day
I read of one who tumbled seven stories
and landed in a neighbor's yard
without a fracture, falling with the unconcern
of one intoxicated (which, as it
later developed, his father was, and in
a rage had thrown him out the window).
But this was so unlikely an occurrence
that no one would believe it in a play.

But take that curious painting by Paul Klee
of Sinbad battling a hostile water,
how strange it seems, how wonderful it is,
a spear too long for one his size to handle,
a boat too small to keep a man afloat,
three variously decorated fishes,
open-jawed but ever held at bay,
flatly emerging from the shades of blue.
No one questions the authenticity.

And oh young lady, barely out of school,
now passing to the outer gallery,
having gazed awhile on Sinbad's critical danger
as if it didn't apply: how can you feel
in this current turn of nights and days
that one day you will die?

CROQUET LOVER
AT THE DINNER TABLE
(at a Writers' Conference)

She passes muffins, orders the most remote
and sudden relishes, comments on
the one particular poem you meant to keep
entirely undiscussed, or interrupts
your train of silence with a stab
of curiosity on what you plan
to do next year if love or money won't
come through, as if it were a game
to find you out: to slam you out of court,
to rout the field, dislodge the set-up shot,
provoke your aim, suggest a change of rules
until you feel immeasurably behind
because her eyes are never wicketed,
dead on nobody and poison to the last.

PASSION OF CROWS

Crows never say much. Maybe an old
one years ago stared at the sun
so long its feathers coaled,
and now they cruise for bits of windblown
silver, odd bits of gold,
whatever glints. When we lay down
young in the forest, we heard their noise.
I held you. I meant to explain
how much I—the words caught down
in my throat—a crow shot from the pine
to look for a little blood on the pineneedles.
And here, I think, began my long decline
into inarticulateness,
it is the crows' and mine.

SUITE

The table folded west
today, the painting back
above it, armchair two-points-south
below the turned settee: holding
this short, affectionate arc.

Often she moves our things around
and around;
she does not lose any of them,
not a one disappears
or goes unsound.

Table lamp, ashtray, scrap basket, books
and vases by degrees are in it,
casting their little score against
the black; and she
   will ask *is it more
   attractive is it more
convenient now?* For a minute

the old way
sits in my eye, like a negative:
This is the new way.
Soon it will be the old way.
It is the way we live.

Perhaps if I concentrate
around one article
and could describe it perfectly—
its declination, pitch,
its character and pole,

and from this whirling allotropy
arrest one part—
perhaps that moment I
would know what is real,
what tears at her heart.

COUNTRY MATTERS

I'm tired of your saying no
you won't get in this hammock with me.
Day's over, dear. We've let the lazy
whitethroat clear his throat and go,
dusk go, and Taurus reappear.
On such a deep blue evening, Zeus
himself as a great snorting bull
came down: the continuity
of all mankind's suggested here.
No worry that we'll drain the sky
in my hammock hung from spruce to spruce,
or a new continent beget.
And yet—your ankles and your wrists,
are they too delicate to know?
The elements of evening sigh
for us, that want you in my net.

BEFORE THE PROPHET
(In the Dark Section with Her Sisters)

"We had gathered, broken and returned
so many times, with our baskets of flowers,
to the leaf-shadowed square, while
he who loved us
lay sick in a high window,
that by now we could hardly remember
how once the air brimmed with invisible wings,
high flutterings the length of our yellow city
over market and fountain, its ribbon of water.
Now dawn silhouetted
only a cynical eastern skyline,
a look of migrations, the streets cleared
and watered for circulation
of trotting carriages from the far stone gates,
and ourselves there, waiting
his cure, and tied for
him to the streets' cold constructions,
where the bells sent over turrets
and pinnacles their recurrent
'No . . . No. . .' until watchmen paced
with lanterns of the evening.

"Soon a frost was dusting the courtyard, the pale chestnut:
and from the hill's high terraced windows
rich ivy looped its fingers,
and our hands were cold.
The city had us, huddled
and bootless, keeping our stations
for a few coins, our baskets full
of poppies, carnations, marigolds,
like piping coals.
              And when news came
that he who had promised us golden sunsets
and the glowing windows of other homes
waiting across the bay, would come, would come—hawks broke,
a black drumbeat, from the citadel."

WATCHERS
(for R.F.)

The curious woods turned out for him;
and sitting soft and wise
in a pine tree at the west room
a winter owl (its eyes
an absolute delirium)
blinks as the old man dies.

Attending him had been a girl
who did not minister.
She drifted in the outer hall
like snow-wind in the fir,
and now the animals on call
return to what they were.

VAN GOGH: *STARRY NIGHT*

Such high, improvident swirls
of ball on yellow ball
of light unwhirling still,
the aspiring town below—
belie his having to descend,
fiercely, into the coal pit,
his coming out
fiercer, to paint the light
behind things: the artist's room,
the tree's irregular bloom.
Nor can it tell
how at the end,
brought to a field of straw
(what is the sun but rings?)
even then he saw
the light behind things.

LOSS OF THE UNICORN
(reincarnated as wood turtle)

Undercover and feeling his
forgotten spike,
no longer really caring
what things are like,

our unicorn stays hard
to capture, even
if girls feel up to it.
Some turtle-haven!—

A sticky terrible wind
had raised the wood
to such a pitch, he headed
out for good,

tiles scrubbed, in character:
dingy-proud
and overserious, like
a small black cloud.

And traveled to a nearby well
circled with stone
and gravel, to find: one flower,
petals turned in.

BELLS
(after *Akenfield*)

Spaces around them, encasing; the way
the clappers fall, and soft tufted sallies;
untumbled, are like banked flames,
suck air from belfries, or seem
to have drunk some darkness vast and friendly,
informal and old. . . . Religious
is too strong and musical too weak
for the change-ringings tolled out over our solitude

in nominals that toss or brood,
sounding the right place, the right time.
This is America. I have never been
obsessed with bells;
but for bellringers of small English villages
they are like architecture, kinship, food.

NOVEMBER

Lifting his head from her thighs
he finds a little snow falling
vertically, first of the year,
history unwinding.
                      And sees,
seeding the air, unlikely
impediments and dyestuff,
pretty enough when there's
a rhythm going for you
1,000 feet above
sea level—and the morning
air is so numinous
life hungers for itself,
itself again, and joy
has risen to this room
that easy lovers keep.
And what is that quickening fringe
of air doing so early
and gentle out there, before
breakfast, unless it is the snow
falling to intercept
a watery shoreline, moving
as tentative in and out,
softly it falls somewhere
irenic, the flurried, headlong
edge of the snow, as off,
snow on the polar penguins
falls, and whitens
the melting polar cap
and the drifting continents
as it falls more faintly
homeward,
                  across day's quaint
geography, her legs
lie open like a wishbone,
and the sun arriving, abrupt.

TIGER LILIES

Always earth holds another
forgiveness at its center:
and tiger lilies splinter

cold air for their own colors,
like teeth or smooth young shoulders,
or the ears that tradewinds bother.

AT HOME

"He sailed upon the seas and waited...."

Those lotuses are my daughters' water wings
floating promiscuously in the pool we bought
from the beaming one-eyed salesman, who only saw
pools in a panic vision, lacking perspective.
Our daughters bob and float, tied to their moons,
until no longer lotuses they, one
by one, run in to you to change.
And while I go on paying by installments
and breezes warm the leaning maple trees,
our pool reflects its hospitality.
Some afternoons a poolless neighbor girl,
after a few noteworthy dives and flounces,
dangles her small, crossed ankles in the water.
I am half-tired, I think, of musing on
her mythological significance.
I let the seasons go—they float
away and back again, as I unwind
at my uprooted beach umbrella, with
a second-rate old fashioned, home too soon
from some essential trip I haven't taken.
I see the downtown twinkle. The pool puts on
its wasting little shades in replica
empty of travelers, as dusk unloads
flowers, puppies. When I head in for supper
I am too easily identified,
the table full of voices, where I stay,
liking the loom you ravel and unravel.

WILLOW STREET

Not far from here it bends, slightly, like tomorrow.
The houses along it, dusk-colored, are mostly square.
Guilt, being only a secret sorrow
over something lost, is not there.

Not far from here, it has no waterfall
or failing wood—
all things returned we still
look forward to, long afterward.

Here the odd, off-center log shifts
and arranges, as stockings depend
innocently again on the hearth, and the drift
will not change from the intended, or end.

TRAVELING WEST

This day, while over hickory a mist
saddens the gray Atlantic, there are young
cones on the hemlock branches, brown of the last,
green of the current year together hung,
as I set off.
         Sputtering still, my scooter
rides by the end of home—its tidy stand
of sugar maple—to alder, pin oak, juniper,
the trembling aspen of burnt-over land,
and swamp, where an ash is blowing. The sun
goes with me (though I miss witch hazel here,
twist-yellow petals and explosions of nut-brown)
deep into autumn, as I become more rare,
into high feathery-headed redwood, learning
to move correctly to a new morning.

WADE'S WAIT (A SEQUENCE)

NOTE:

Chuck Wade is a private detective. In an earlier, unrelated poem, he introduced himself this way:

> *Warm night alone,*
> *I stare*
> *again at my dusty*
> *two-bulb chandelier,*
>
> *a Holmes without his*
> *Watson. Just burned in*
> *on the wind's roulette*
> *below my screen*
>
> *a sidekick June bug is*
> *playing her cards right,*
> *and her singing leg*
> *tonight*
>
> *floats over my thin*
> *scholarship and library*
> *to admit herself*
> *like me, a solitary.*
>
> *I too am essentially*
> *mobile and cannot help*
> *answering almost any*
> *appeal for help,*
>
> *and appreciate her*
> *stopping to send up*
> *a low-down song from her crucible*
> *and carry me to sleep. . . .*

As this present collection begins Wade is 31, just back from European assignments, and better off than he used to be.

LUSTINGS
(Time: the late 'forties)

It was mid spring. Nothing much had happened
in the farm town of Mackson, Wisconsin,
all winter. Almost everything went on
too long, they agreed, including winter.
Beyond a brief flurry of excitement
over the burning of the lumberyard
in August, winter allowed its quota
of petty smalltown gossip and intrigues
to keep things tolerable—a few deaths
by old age, some unwanted pregnancies,
the usual knee-deep snowfalls and drifts
and wind; so many long gray days.
Then comes a thaw. A warm wind. Suddenly
there comes a charitable sky at night
as if, blown back, the season remembers
you after all, and earth is welcoming.
On one spring night, past midnight, a figure
of medium height moved along Main Street
in a tan overcoat, lapel turned up,
face hidden by a visored cap, passing
unnoticed, carrying a paper bag.
The sky, part overcast, carried small clouds
adrift, moon showing sporadically.
At one point a little mutt scrambled out
from his hiding place under a store front
and scurried to the feet of the figure,
whose steady pace didn't acknowledge him.
The dog, deflated, stood looking after,
and then, trotting back, nosed under the store.
The walker headed down a dirt sideroad.
At the end of the road lay a wide field.
Unused, it had long grass, but still winter's
grass. It was like an ocean with dark waves.
Directly the person struck across it.
At the far edge of it another road
came down from woods to end in a clearing
before trees, a stand of empty buildings:

an old farmhouse, its northern roof caved in,
and several scattered sheds, an outhouse,
a barn without doors, where the person stopped
and stood, appearing to listen—much as
the little dog had done—before taking
a bottle from the paper bag, and poured—
exactingly, with a languid design—
liquid along the base and window sills
and front wall of the farmhouse; and stepped back.
Then a match came arcing through the air. It
caught. Like a burst of water the flame sprang
to the sideboards and up. Shoots of brightness
took the foreground. Suddenly the farmhouse
was all heat and crackle, a watery
music, like little cups of fire falling
into themselves, that have always sought
death and must drop into it; and the flames
lit up the face, too, of this gazer who
had leapt behind a bush and was crouching,
her eyes slightly dilated. She had high
cheekbones, a small chin, a slanting forehead,
intent and somewhat angular features.
She was lean, rather than really pretty.
She hardly moved. The light from the farmhouse
illuminated the road behind it,
old posts running uphill. A small attic
window filled with yellow, the roof taking.
Something else inside cracked heavily, fell;
branches overhead were singed, sparked, as she
crouched at the low bushes where a few sparks
floated to the ground, breathing more and more
quickly. Her body shivered—then relaxed.
She removed her gloves. Pulling the coat
around her, she slowly took the same path
through the grass, pausing midway to inspect
the conflagration, then turned, continued
across the field. The animals watched her.

It took Wade a few moments to know where he was again,
    the snug room,
a single window half-open. His dream drifted. It
    was night outside,
with lights spinning along his ceiling, a red, a blue flashing,
    and a wail of sirens. He leapt
to the window in time, of course, to miss everything. The
    street was empty,
though an unnatural glow softened the sky off left, above
    the uneven rooftops and skyline.

Wade had rolled into Mackson that morning—or rather
    been towed in,
his faithless Condatti offering another lesson against
    bringing
obscure European models back from the Continent.
    Today
it broke down again, eight miles outside Mackson, and the
    mechanics,
all ceremoniously sympathetic, couldn't hope to diagnose it
    before Monday.
But these mishaps might be telling him something, that maybe
    he ought
to slow down? he was pushing himself and the car too hard?

    Maybe I ought to slow down,

he wrote in his journal, pulled up at the table's
    oversized lamp—once awake
he needed to tire himself out before falling asleep
    again,
his mind was that active (he liked to think). But he
    had slowed down.

    I came swinging off
    the 4-lane this morning to see
    some farm areas, only not this much.

*All kinds of potholes—winter
had been rough on these roads,
or else the tar was poured cold,
not hot. But a fine time, being
a day ahead of myself. Spring
made everything smell fresh,
I was spinning along listening
to Mozart (early, but excellent)
with my elbow out the window,
the wind blowing over my elbow,
tanning it, let's say, when this funny
noise started up in the motor
like a pebble jumping around,
then a blue dashlight went on, one
of those international signals
you need your manual for.*

Everything caught up, didn't it? Old thoughts, memories, things
    you bought that shouldn't be
uprooted, like this car, but always, each year, this easy
    déjà-vu quality
of spring. It warmed you, blending into the night,
    encouraging dreams.
What was that dream he'd been having? His first home:
    afternoon sunlight
slanted on a long clear lawn. He was a boy now,
    barefooted, dashing through
the sprinkler. Some women moved on the lawn to an
    unfamiliar music.

*   I felt
very stupid standing at the side
of the road with my beauty,
but finally a pick-up jounced by
and I hitched in—a retired farmer,
a wiry and talkative old boy. Been born
in Mackson, raised in Mackson,*

*worked all his life and retired
in Mackson since he liked the place.
His pick-up smelled of corn somehow.
He dropped me at a garage, the best
in town he said. With three
mechanics, except weekends naturally,
given my luck. A rather
spiffy blonde on the books.
Overall, an easy-going lot,
nobody there understood my car's
trouble, or seemed very eager to.
Tonight—well, I took a few beers
downstairs and simply watched a
bargirl squirting Pabst on draft
into mugs, how first she'd squirt
a long sideways one, letting the head
rise, then a quick follow-up just
to the top with no foam spill.
Watching her was more instructive
than drinking them down.*

Given his headache, too, he'd scribbled enough for the time,
    and dull stuff at that.
He returned to bed, read part of a thriller, and lay there.
    It was still night.
He'd double-checked the horizon off left, the same as
    before or brighter,
and obviously a problem for somebody, but Wade was no
    accident or
catastrophe chaser, he rarely cared about such things
    unless someone died.

        . . . by grass, darkness,
streetlights, reaching the upper door she'd left
unlocked. Set back, attaching to the house,

a flight of wooden steps ran up to it,
a platform at the top, where she waited
gazing a few moments at the far glow;
then pushed the door open. A thin hallway
of creaky boards required quietness.
From a windowseat near the hall closet
one could see a treed backyard area
mostly in shadow. She looked down,
not as if she feared somebody was there,
but more as if she needed to. She put
her hat and coat away, catching a few
hangers before they rattled, as the door
to the bathroom opened, and her father,
stooped over slightly, his thin hair ruffled:

"Anna—what's the matter? What's going on?"

Each was clearly startled by the other.
She stood there in day-clothes, startled, wearing
a summer cotton dress and blue sweater.
Hatless, she appeared smaller than before.

"I—well—I was about to take a walk,
I can't sleep. I thought maybe some air, or. . . ."

"But you're all right? Everything's all right?"

"I'm fine, just wakeful. I think I'll just go
back to bed and read something for a while."

And opened the door to her bedroom: here
everything in it looked suspended
by a gray light, cool, even the bookcase,
various books tilted or piled sideways,
magazines spilling from the bottom shelf.
Before a full-length mirror, she took off
her clothes and laid them over the chairback,

      then slid her pillow off the bed and lay
      down naked on the bed, on her stomach,
      resting one hand at the small of her back,
      the other hung from the bedside, her eyes
      open a short time before she closed them.

Wade wandered near the ashes, humming. Some had blown
    down or drifted
loosely onto the trees, branches with spring leaves.
    Well, the firehouse bunch
left a soggy mess of things. But had stopped a fire
    that, with a little wind
or inattention, might have taken the woods and spread
    townward.
Perhaps the small crowd felt this, and it lent a light
    tension he felt in the air.
An odd place for a fire—of course, there was always a
    reason for everything.
A few townspeople eyed him, in fact, as the sporty stranger
    among them; suspicion
might even fall his way. "They'll have a hard time proving
    anything,"
he reflected, his mind jumping, as usual, some pointless
    steps ahead.

At an edge of the Sunday gathering stood the old gentleman
    who'd brought
him into town yesterday and given him the bum steer
    on garages.
Too late to duck him. Looking chatty and eager, he was
    already approaching Wade,
who seemed to attract such people, rather than the quieter
    ones he preferred.

So Wade got the story. This whole area had been abandoned
    for years, ever since the surviving

son moved into town—that short fellow over there beside
    the investigator picking through debris. Quite a scattering
    of fires in the last year, this was no accident either.
    Useless property, really. You'd have needed a new
    homestead anyhow, and town water. The expense. And what
    would you do
with it, in this spot? Wade shifted feet. He'd noticed
    a fuzzy blueness,
possibly wood violet, the state flower, running below the
    untouched eastern trees,
some fantasy was shaping itself in his head: the birds,
    the open setting,
the dry woods, engaging in their quaint way, he could see
    a simple half-modern structure
aimed to the view, nicely detached from town. Though he
    wanted to get away. A rasping
caught in the man's throat as he talked, the way a
    silencer sounds
like a penny hitting water at a certain angle.

        . . . and it was hard getting away,

he wrote, after a change of socks, having no other shoes.
    A wet glove
lay on the table before him. He enjoyed doing this journal
    for reasons
he'd never quite settled, this casual running bridge between
    himself and the world.

        I walked back, a nice shortcut
        through the field, but unwise maybe,
        with its grass very long and dewy.
        Though I found a half-evident path
        bending the right way. Actually
        I enjoyed the wet grass against my
        legs, the loose feel of it, the air,
        birds singing, like the old days

*when my father and I went birding
together in summers. I miss him,
I miss them both. About halfway
I found a work glove lying to the left,
not very deep in the grass, resting.
It's a fairly new one, or at least
not dirty, with a faint earth smell,
but also the smell of gasoline.
Which I note down reluctantly,
since this trip, after all, was meant
to be different, was meant to be
my vacation.*

Anna came down early that Sunday
and opened the front door of the drugstore
and gathered up the bundled newspapers
and putting them on the table cut strings
with her knife and set eleven copies
below the counter for her regular
customers. Already it was a bright
morning. She had eaten breakfast quickly
and dressed before her father and, downstairs,
uncovered the canary who began
to primp, jump, sing a little, as ever.
She sat on a stool behind the counter
leaning on one elbow, flicking pages
of *Photoplay* backward through the gossip
section. The sunlight fell on her knuckles.

Finished and wanting a smoke, with no cigars in his
    suitcase sideflaps,
Wade wandered up Main Street. Stratus clouds
lay over the trees; it would be raining before
    nightfall.

He had returned from Europe too soon. He had left
	behind
the music of Europe. His best cases, the answers to
	everything. And those winding
roads through mountains, antique hillsides, arches,
	the geometry of
pools in Oslo reflecting big purple trees, all Europe
	catching up
after the war, like his thought. Like his thought
	the clouds today
stretched sideways into emptying wisps of imaginings,
	throwbacks.
Well, he'd had to come home sometime. Throw of the dice.
	His own country,
like an inheritance, rangy and loose and open, wanting
	a new language.
It was just that, once home, he'd committed himself
	too quickly
to deRochemont, who needed him clear on the coast by
	midweek, which now looked impossible.

Not that this town required you long, as the painted
	sign said,

And a pleasant town, as small towns go, although on
	Sunday everything
shut except church. This street he walked along
	tossed up its informal
and settled midcentury ease that, sentimentally,

                    he liked,
a counterpoint, in these transitional days, to his
            near rogue-life.
Or maybe it was the lazy energetic sunlight of
            spring that made things
so full of themselves, happy to be there. Wade's
            shoulders relaxed,
he was carried down a sidestreet without knowing
            why precisely.
Here he found a mingling of shops and detached houses
            running downhill
with no fixed design: baked houses in sunlight, some
            weather-beaten tiles
needing repair. Small gardens. A clotheshorse of
            very casual
underwear lifting in the breeze. And, after these things,
            an open drugstore.
And the shop was laid out modestly in two aisles,
            a wall for the pulps and glossies;
a canary sang as he opened the door, with its overhead
            tinkle, but stopped abruptly.

A girl sat behind a glassed counter containing cigars
            in closed and open boxes, along with tins of
            imported tobacco. Dark hair
just reached her shoulders, her mouth was unpainted. Small.
            With a jolt, he remembered
another woman crossing the Ponte Vecchio in Florence, very
            much like this one, if slightly older,
it was the end of day, dusk, rather breezy also, the warm
            hour when people are leaving work heading home or back
            to lovers. The Arno
lay yellow-brown in the late sun. At one end of the bridge
            stood an old beggar
selling pencils and shoelaces. And from the crowd, as if
            torn loose, or fragmentary, came this pretty dark-haired

   woman in a white blouse with ruffles, shouldering her
   trim purse of brown, gold-buttoned Florentine leather.
   She looked oddly rushed or distracted,
and their eyes had met, embarrassingly, for an instant
   as she hurried past. He had never forgotten her.

Now in Mackson, dawdling, he continued to read the box
   label he'd asked,
after several others, to examine, "Not to be sold for
   less than...."

The air in the shop seemed stuffy, muffled. Church bells
   began to ring
uproad, with a flat sound. He'd also be needing some
   toothpaste soon,
but only the small-sized toothpaste, he hated those
   big money-saving tubes.

     —And how did you happen to get such a varied
   selection, Wade asked the girl.

     —My father runs the store, she said, briefly
   but not coldly.

He studied the layout further, hoping for complications.
   The girl, hands at her sides,
had the instinctive, streetwise look he always recognized
   and liked,
though he lacked it himself, and he sensed, half-pleasantly,
   her body when she moved,
her animal breasts under the blouse, slight nub of nipples.
   It had been a long time.
So much running around after answers, finding a reason
   for everything (his passion
yes, his long need and fascination) but a
   romance
could drop out of things? Go by? No time to stop,

     to settle. He'd have liked
to touch her then, gently, touch her with a kindly
     protective touch.
She, in turn, seemed just to be studying his shoes,
     still wet.

      —Now this brand, he said, these little Danish ones,
   are they fairly mild, or wouldn't you know?

      —I wouldn't know. Do you want to buy one?
   She had grown petulant under her thin smile.

Something, a chance passed easily, slipped away;
     he looked up.

They weren't what he wanted. He bought the box anyhow.
     Also a Sunday paper
for the long afternoon, although news was the last thing
     he needed.

It was then as he turned in the doorway, cupping his
     match flame
against a quick breeze, that he caught her eyes, rather
     opaque, fixing him
over the flame, through the flame, and startled
     a second time,
he paused just a moment too long for the casual stance
     he'd meant to affect.

      After she heard her father snoring, she
      slipped down the outer staircase into the
      warm night. The clouds had scattered, sending no
      rain after all. She walked along Main Street.
      As her way bent left, downhill, and sidewalks
      and shops dwindled to houses where the lawns

    or low hedges directly met the road,
    she stopped at the second house. It was dark,
    just an unshaded bulb on, casting a
    diagonal to the attached workshop,
    which she entered. In shadow were some rakes,
    a toy wheelbarrow, maybe a half-cord
    of maple, randomly piled newspapers.
    She stood awhile there, hesitating and
    breathing quietly, holding the matches.
    Then left. Passing the town hotel she glanced
    up. There were no signs of activity.

Sometimes he wondered—as he did the next evening, Monday,
    away from Mackson—
why the timing of things mattered so much. He'd been
    surprised
before noon, idly checking the garage, to find his Condatti
    finished and ready to go.
He tried to conceal his disappointment. The idea of spare
    days in Mackson
had been growing on him, and with no excuse now, morally
    he should yield
to deRochemont and move on. But the car looked dirty,
    less flashy
than usual. He asked for a wash, while he headed back
    to pack up.

Then a bigger surprise: on reaching his room, he found it
    tidied
and the bed made, but the glove, which he'd left on the
    table, had vanished.
Quickly he searched the room. He wanted that glove.
    He'd been thinking—
vaguely, as a hunch—of ways to test the girl with it.
    In a way, she haunted him.

It was silly, but he could enter the shop with the glove
    dangling from his pocket . . .
or he could wear it on one hand . . . or place it on the counter
    while buying toothpaste?
Well, no matter now. With deRochemont waiting, he could
    hardly justify
sticking around on a groundless hunch, glove or no glove.
    Throw it in. Forget the glove.

Still, he asked about it downstairs.
As he heard their answers, watching their confusion,
    he began to feel
sheepish: an old work glove, why would these people have
    taken it? And the girl,
even supposing her guilty, how would she get the glove,
    or know it was there,
or want it back, even? Why not throw the other one out?
    Well, no,
he imagined she had it back. One way or another, he'd been
    quietly taken at his own game.

It didn't make sense. Her face haunted him. Several
    times he debated
dropping into the store again anyhow, but thought
    better of it.

He found a pleasant, small roadside hotel near evening
    on the scruffy
edge of somewhere three hundred miles, maybe, west of
    Mackson,
and after a fine steak at the neighboring diner,
    continued,

It didn't make sense.
The manager called his daughter
over who'd done my room, the same
bar girl I'd been watching on my

first night, only a kid by day,
gumchewing, very ingenuous, hard not
to believe her. She hadn't seen
any glove. Soon we were all
rummaging wherever she'd cleaned,
into laundry piles, the wife too,
like a down-and-out vaudeville team.
I felt pretty sorry I'd asked
by now, since I kept picturing
the road ahead, happy to get away,
as I did finally—the best weather
for traveling, and the Condatti, I'll say,
behaved beautifully again, as I'd known
it would, after its usual
initial warm-up, the radio playing
and window down, as we threw
the first miles behind us, a sweet thing
on the turns doing fifty. . . .

But he felt off-stride with a rhythm broken, having
    ended up
somehow in the wrong place, the wrong town, and he put
    the still-open
journal aside, temporarily, as something that didn't
    bear thinking
about just then. His youth was gone.

DINNER WAS SERVED
(25 years later)

Wade's journal

i

Warm night alone.
After so many years
off-work I take up
my pen again

to begin another
journal. I have thrown
everything out, forgotten
everything I've known.

Nearly forgotten my
grubbing for justice down
those flickering unjust days
to a kind of song.

Forgotten what friends I had.
Now suddenly I'm called back—
and although I may enjoy
seeing Gregory next week

somehow I can't terribly
care about saving him.
No, the old days
play out, and while I'm

quieter,
easier than before,
I don't hear
that song anymore.

ii

The rain was letting up,
my deSoto rattling down the foggy
tree-lined drive to a turn-around
loop at Gregory's house,
a Colonial sea-fronter, aloof
by night, vaguely a mustard yellow.
A single porch light only
suggested the lawns. Small roses
on the rosa rugosa filling the loop-center looked
like bruises. I heard
sea behind the house.

He must have been watching for my
headlights through the rain for hours,
for suddenly he stood on the dim
porch, lit by the overhead,
a frail if dapper figure for sixty, bent
by his old war injury and holding
an ivory cane I remembered now
from his father. The old days
were coming back. We sat
in the long kitchen nursing our differences: milk
for his ulcer, a double nightcap for me.

And reviewed, of course, the blackmail
business. He explained
how the people themselves, by unhappy
coincidence, were sleeping upstairs,
too late to have warned me on the road.
Then showed me an ocean
room: sidetable, lamp, old book
of anecdotes for the wakeful, which I wasn't,
a soap dish with folded
towels on a twin bed, a triangular
half-bath adjoining.

We shook hands in the doorway, smiling
excessively I felt,
his tapering hand worn smooth
as if by greetings. Clearly
he needed something,
and that's where I came in.
As waves pounded the rocks below,
my head full of the traveling day,
I lay in bed thinking
of old jokes, thinking
my whole life was a cliché.

iii

Maybe the whiskey
wearing off,
maybe a noise
or the moonlight

woke me. A sharp
moon dropped a ripple
to the inlet, anyhow,
and the open sea and islands.

Lightheaded, I shuffled
over to look,
then on to the little bathroom
to piss. When I came out

somebody stood in the doorway.
I would have preferred
nobody. But Harriet had
that way of appearing.

"I thought I heard someone—hello,"
she said, lightly
fingering her negligee.
"Gregory's asleep, like a top."

Too neat, maybe?
As she leaned forward to kiss
me hello, an extended
shatter and clump

sounded downstairs, then
a door swung in the hallway,
more doors, and emerging heads
of other light sleepers.

What we found in the pantry
was no picnic—the butler
crumpled, his dropped tumbler
trailing a crescent of milk.

iv

His body lay in a mess.
A dutiful gentleman
in a state of half undress.
He had tried to grip the drain
board, tipping tea cups and saucers
and assorted silverware going down,
his flimsy silk pajamas
ripped half open.
He kept, nevertheless,
an air of just carrying on
as old butlers will, his face
perfectly dull as if he'd been
dead for years, the innocuous
snake slipping its skin.

v

My visit seemed to be
getting off on the wrong foot,
wrong but predictable,
whenever I go out, some sort
of trouble follows me.
You gentle folks
at home romanticize a gumshoe's
walk of life
who think it's kiss and kill.
No, no—more like a drawer of socks,
forever unscrambling your darks
and lights without a wife,
then all this
walking on goddam tiptoes.

vi

Of course at breakfast
it fell on me to check
these relatives out who'd just
arrived a day before me,
who made an extended family
of four (beyond our host
and circulating hostess).
Naturally I did my best
to like them, one
does what one can
even at such a hazy hour
as they sat working to look
alert and blameless,
a string of pearls for sure.

Just to my right
Jud was the first pearl, hardly
real or cultured, as unlike
his older brother Gregory
as you could have it.
But he found himself okay—
muscular, dark, and woolgathering
with a sort of tacked-on gloom
as if he'd typically play
the life of the party or nothing.
In this case nothing. No use
to make conversation, no use to stick
a fingerbowl in front of him
as Harriet had done, by habit.

Beside him, Jackie his wife
was a warm little fanfare blonde,
hospitality was her long suit,
suggesting in her indiscriminate
wish to please everyone

and the surrealistic get-up of her face
something beyond hospitality:
like a deep hole, oblivion.
Once, in my faraway, cut-off
youth, I could have fancied this,
but no longer—such dizzy
blue-chip eyes, like roulette
balls bouncing from slot
to slot, a world beyond.

Jumping from Jackie and Jud
on the family stem—
Gregory's daughter Pat was almost too
top-heavy, if that can be,
her sweater made it hard
to keep your eyes entirely off them.
She spoke in whispers without any
point or style,
she loved her scrambled eggs,
she found the coffee good,
her rejoinders, since she tended to
repeat whatever was said and smile,
at least added nothing new
(while I speculated on her legs).

In his cashmere v-neck
and tennis racquet tie, her Harry was
like your willowy English dandy
of another decade, sporty
and trophy-oriented, always "on top
of things," though he coughed a lot
in the air still cool and foggy,
a morning for catarrhs.
It was quite a mystery
how Pat and Harry could ever live
together, with her endless smiles, his not
very dry or engaging wit

darting at intervals to make
even his silences competitive.

So there it was, a morass
of relatives, Gregory's
sulking brother Jud and wife
Jackie; his daughter Pat
and husband Harry
and the group of them
all gathered round like a mildly
strangling necklace,
though hardly, from where I sat,
showing sparkle and spunk enough
for anything awful or great—
they looked simply inconsiderate,
this being the cook's week off
and untimely to visit.

vii

I hadn't slept since Gregory first
shuffled us back to bed refusing
to phone the police or doctor (let's think
about it, he said) and I lay dutifully
in bed thinking about it until
the light came through. And crept down.
I couldn't claim to be the tough guy
of my youth, but I felt an old thrill
returning, the sheer necessity
to see if the layout could betray
anything.

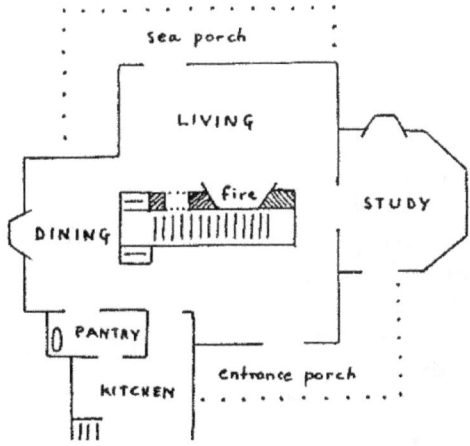

    Nobody up. And quite
an odd family to take catastrophe
so lightly. But a pleasantly airy,
circular home with nice touches—
a games-closet cut through the stairwall
with doors of leaded glass to let

you look through into a living room.
Almost nothing contemporary. A lot
of fireplaces. The dining room suite
showed a copper samovar and Canton
china, walnut sideboard with rosy
cut-glass decanter and snifters on it,
all from the days of limitless faith
and light when Gregory's father built—
I felt his kind, downreaching hand
in this. Oddly, it made me hungry.
But considering events I didn't care
to rifle the refrigerator for snacks
when I looked in. The new milk carton
that Gregory had opened and returned
to the top shelf was gone. It lay
in the trash, empty. I smelled the lip:
the unmistakable smell of James's
tumbler, when Harry had stooped to finger-
sample the spill and I'd restrained him.
A clue, anyhow. I went outside
and wandered a while, I just thought
I ought to. Everything dripped. Light fog
was drifting in, the soaked lawns showed
nothing, no prints in the flowerbeds
or by windows or on porches (except
my own) to suggest visitors. A lobster boat
chugged invisibly in fog. Already
I felt a loosening to the scenery
overnight, the late spring moving to
summer, season of my own wife, dead
these seven years. I went back. Later
Harriet announced that earlier, lying
drowsy in bed and half-asleep
before the big noise, she'd possibly heard
somebody out on the upper landing
and creak of the upper stair, but maybe
not, maybe it was a dream.

viii

In the study, Gregory muttered,
"Well, even letting a doctor see him,
who might require an autopsy,
and then reporters—" he glanced sideways,
tamping tobacco with a silver tamper.
James's blanketed body lay out
on a tufted gold settee, a Victorian
leftover at the roadside window,
shade down. "I'd been maintaining
a lower profile lately, Chuck.
That's why I called you in, really."

I waited. "You were expecting this?"

"Sweet Jesus no, I mean the old
trouble between Jud and me.
Always this stupid trouble between
my brother and me. The way he's never
accepted—" Gregory waved his match hand,
letting the flame go out— "all this.
I mean, how *I* was Father's favorite.
Or maybe just the older, who knows
how Father really felt? Anyway,
Jud got his bundle, simply not
this summer house. And didn't keep
what he did get, either. Damn this pipe. . . .
And now last month the boy announces
he's dug up something on me, he
and Harry too, they both have."

                                            "What
have they dug up on you, Gregory?"

"I'd rather not go into that
today, as I said before," his words

slurring a bit. He'd opened up
a specialty from his old reserve,
quite fruity. Serving wine just now
seemed rather inappropriate,
but anyhow. "The thing I want
is a counterjab from you, bargaining,
counterblackmail, whatever it takes.
I'd meant, you know, to keep this weekend
free for our initial chat.
I didn't mean to make you meet
them all so soon."

                    "My pleasure," I said.
"This troupe was totally unexpected?"

"An hour's warning—can you believe it,
all of them on the road already,
and the cook gone, too? The cook, you see,
she names her week, and Harriet and I
make do for that period. Obviously
we're not set up to entertain.
At least these crazy relatives!
Jud—he's been irrational
since birth, always feisty and jealous
simply at being the younger brother,
always the rakehell dragging in
one floozy after another. Jackie's
his seventh try, you know—I hate
to imagine the alimony. As for
Harry, he chiseled his way into
the family and took my Pat away
for the money, as I often told her,
and finally she's admitting. God,
if I could just report this thing
I'd do it, but we'd need an angle,
a story we could all stick to.
You'd never get it with this crowd.

Jud calls me an accessory.
Jackie's upstairs vomiting,
apparently something she brought with her.
Harry's running around complaining.
Except for my poor Pat, I'd call
them all a bunch of damned freeloaders.
I know this doesn't sound like me."

It did, though. His gentility
ran thin, I remembered, years ago
when our two fathers knew each other.
(James I'd considered exemplary.)

"I called you in," he said, "because
you're good. Professional, a friend."

"I'm rusty."

        "Never mind, we've got
a problem," he said, eyeing the sofa,
his voice dropping, and poured himself
a freshener—you couldn't miss
the hand trembling—"a real problem."
He looked at me. "And who do you
suppose was the *intended* victim?"

"I—wouldn't call that one."

        The long
afternoon, as the sun sank over
to the far side of the house,
had begun to cool and darken slightly
his small study, sombering
some off-the-ceiling greenery,
Harriet's touch. It was not
unpleasant. In the wiggly panes
I could see far whitecaps running

to funny blips and leaps—and I also
found the distortions not unpleasant,
the way in some boring situations
a sudden corpse invigorates one,
like a stain—like the way great Leonardo,
when he had nothing doing, used to
study the dampness stains on walls
for inspiration.

                "I'm scared," he said.
"My goddam life is slipping away.
It must be obvious I'm scared.
Talk, Chuck! You don't say anything."

"Well . . . if Jud and Harry wanted money,
why would they kill you, Gregory,
with your Harriet inheriting?
How would that help? Still, I agree,
poisoning milk would hardly seem
a likely way to kill a butler."

"No. But, dammit, it's possible,
if we're just talking *method*. James—
I'm making a connection now—
had developed some insomnia
since Father died, he often came
down late to get warm milk and crackers.
And everyone knew it! The poor man,
he just got quirkier and more lackluster
over the years—I guess he loved
my father like a one-man dog.
We'd let him wander anywhere
around the house, tidying things.
We liked to give him the free run."

"Got on with the cook?"

                          "Oh, sure.
Professional, no more, no less.
She's young and saucy, out of his league.
Not much of a cook, either."

No tipoffs coming through. Or mixed
signals. Our conversation moving
toward silence, as things tend to.

"A generally fine fellow, then?"

Gregory gestured—his pipe and wine
had blurred him sentimentally.
"Yes, yes, the sort of help you can't
get nowadays, he sensed whatever
you needed, he knew everything.
Even the timing here is such
a shame, since he was planning to
retire this fall, go back to Scotland.
Or maybe not a shame—for *us*.
If people ask, we'll say he's back
to Scotland, it's our simplest out!"

My host's demeanor underwent
a false brightening. I tried again:
"But shouldn't we report this now?"

His answer—quick and edgy, "Too late,
I tell you, it's too late."

ix

Going downstairs for supper I met
him halfway on the rise,
Jud glaring at me, a gruff hand
on the banister,
nobody spoke. A pause.

"Whoever you are, pal, whatever
you're doing here,
this is family stuff—if you
could move, please?"

Okay, I moved.
As the feller says, never
complain, never explain,
never apologize.

x

Night, at last I am
off smoking. Room lights off.
The bickering crowd all off
to bed. My cigar tastes
poor, it is too old.
Or am I too old?

The old smoke, feathers in the room's
moonlight, against a flowered
wallpaper, seems to be
a real object moving. It's not.

Oh, well. What am I
thinking? I need to think
of her again, near summer now,
how finally I am her
age, nearly, when she died.

How all I do,
how even the journal I write,
these wandering stories and songs, I do
for her, to reach her,
she moves me forward, this narrow line we
play here, the—

my window open for smoke
or I wouldn't have heard
the shuffle.
         Below, at the porch,
came two figures, three really,
or, better, a single shape tangled and
shifting crablike into the driveway,
Gregory and his brother Jud
and a blanketed bundle wrapped in a sort
of netting bag, like a snood,

with Gregory handling the bent
end, himself limping,
they edged to the open trunk
of the Mercedes.
Then Gregory shut the lid, a click,
their getaway decently quiet,
with hardly a pebble crunch,
leaving all that suddenly absurd
emptiness, or so it appeared
absurd now, the empty
road and stone gateway,
the rosa rugosa bush, clumps, trees,
rock masses in moonlight. I felt
a hand on my shoulder. I swung.
"He woke me leaving," she said,
"he didn't realize. You know what this means."
"No, Harriet." She stood in her same
negligee, the light shadowing
her small breasts, an aristocrat's.
"Help me"—a new voice from her.
"You'll smell of cigar
if you stay," I said—pointlessly;
"also, you're married."
She waited. "It's a sham.
He hasn't touched me in years,
he doesn't love me, nobody
in this house loves anybody,"
and then, as we heard the car
downshifting back here later ,
it was over, she drifted out
taking her long legs with her.

xi

Breakfast, nobody spoke
anymore—a click
of silverware, cups, and plates
that once were the good gentleman's
who built this house,
and, munching quietly,
sat all the old boy's progeny
about to strike,
each one eyeing the others. Once,
I suppose, in Italy
the Borgia branch was even worse,
but any family hits
its peak
and then declines.

xii

It finally came
to me later that morning
as I sat in the bathtub
humming an old tune,
a frayed hooked rug
under the tubfeet,
wall clock ticking,
sun through the window,
hearing the wash
of sea on the craggy
rocks far and away,
and feeling this case
was hardly a feather
in my cap—as I pulled
the fluted tin soap dish
along the tub rail
and soaped a little:
Warm milk and crackers
Gregory had said
the butler took.
Then—why wasn't the
milk warm that fell?
Not even slightly?
And why was I waiting
in this tub?

xiii

And that was the way I came to
the last room, after so long. Maybe I knew
what to expect, a simplicity and spare
esthetic.
          One rocker, book bent open.
Window overlooking some older fir
trees, side view to the sea, and through
his open dormer floated a sense of the sea air.
Bedcovers were thrown back
as he had left them, wide.
So then he went downstairs and died?
Well, yes. But an oversight to have left
the alarm clock set for 2:00.
I thought a while. I thought, and with
my handkerchief I set the alarm ahead.

Then to the top drawer—underwear,
cuff-links, handkerchiefs, silk socks,
some paper boxes and mementos,
and finally, along with these, a vial
of powder scrapings,
he hadn't used it all.

Only enough to slip
away, leaving us all to
ourselves at last, leaving me here to hide
his secret now? as from below
came up the freshening endless cries of anger,
arguing. I pocketed
the poison. Let the chips fall
where they would. I was satisfied.

POOL SHOT
(five years later)

> "Pool is like the violin—you've got to play an hour every day."
> —Sonny Greer, drummer for Duke Ellington

1

Wade was out of work, but that was no
different. He had a kind of dog-eared look
settling about him. Nobody noticed—
that is, noticed the difference. Much of his time
he spent sitting at the outdoor café
the Carrenton Hotel had fashioned itself
when the city redid its walks and planted trees
in pebbled circles with little wire fences
around their bases, rather continental.
He sat under an umbrella. It was a warm
summer then, sunnier than usual,
And fine for sitting outside before dark
away from traffic and pedestrians
if you liked that: waiters circulated
unobtrusively, napkins over their wrists,
a pleasant flavor and flair spread over
that area of town bordering the old
slums and their gradual renovations,
and Wade with deliberate counter-seediness,
sipping Pernod or white wine, was looking
continental, I thought, as if he found it
his way of being inwardly fashionable.
Something, anyhow, satisfied him. Although
his clothes looked like the end of a career,
still his demeanor, studied, curious,
even over-casual, said don't be fooled.
He couldn't quite be measured. Maybe he really
was on the downward spiral his dress implied,
and possible tipsiness. He wasn't always
there, but I never saw him leaving either.
I can't say if he left a tip.
                            Sometimes
I'd take a walk I wouldn't otherwise have,
strolling at random. Other afternoons,

taking an indirect way to the car,
I'd pass the Carrenton to check him out
and usually find him sitting there, alone.
My irritation grew. I liked to assume
he didn't see me—at least our glances
never met, since I would single him
out from a distance, and if he shifted
or showed signs of looking up, I'd look away.
It was all pretty clean.
                      Then, if I drove
home thinking about it, his effrontery,
his placid assurance of dropping into
such ease, I'd flop into my own armchair
without wanting to move sometimes for hours.
The empty house was like a cold hand now.
I didn't need to light up the whole thing.
Usually I'd retire to the den
and run the table. Something to do.... Three lights
over the green felt, in green shades, were just
my way of staying consciously old-style.
Slowly I was becoming rather accomplished,
clearing my mind. Once in mid-July
Wade wasn't there for three afternoons running,
but then appeared again same as ever.
The routine bothered me—the break, I mean.
Later I played past midnight, keeping the game
slower and more methodical, I remember,
angling each ball carefully or feathering it,
because the other way, that night, they didn't
drop easily. My topspin was off.

Actually my wife was too smalltown
to take the house, her ingenuity
being the facts she'd gathered up against me.
In the first months I counted myself lucky,
no terrible loser. Then the house began
to get lonelier, pictures, furniture, all

the paraphernalia one is left over with.
Worse—at the office, opening a drawer,
I found the anniversary bracelet
I'd bought a year ago, and when I lit
my pipe and spread the bracelet out to admire
the workmanship (meaning to wrap the thing
myself I hadn't let the shopgirl wrap it),
I saw its beauty again—a dozen oval stones
banded by silver, each with sidebands flaring
out like tiny sheephorns, the tip ends
curled into circles for delicate linking chains
of silver, all with a slightly muted buff
setting the oxblood coral off. The pain
ran through me. Like sheephorns, were they? No,
not really, but a faint association
touched me then, as on the day I'd bought it,
something to do with the farms of our childhoods,
orchards, cattle, sheep, buzzing of crickets,
like the first moment I knew I loved her,
I was lying in bed—and it was raining,
a cool light rain, maybe spring, maybe fall,
whatever the season I was about twelve,
and the patter started just before bedtime,
overhead, windless, not against my window,
and I could hear it on the trees outside,
on the leaves, so it wasn't winter I know.
The feeling came from nowhere, the open sound
of rain lifting us, stretching us all out.
The rain was cheerful and sad and mysterious.
Then suddenly it struck me rain was falling
on her roof, too, exactly a mile away,
and I laughed aloud. Those were the days
I often laughed aloud just before sleep.
I never really knew what brought it on.
My laugh simply hung there in the dark.
It might come anytime, unexpectedly—
I might be only mulling the day over,

or watching winter stars, watching, guessing
the pretty constellations over our town,
the way things had to be, a tacit but
inevitable circle. I suppose my sense
of inevitability came early, from prayers
and dotty relatives. Before grade school
I'd got astrology and the zodiac signs
from Aunt Louise, my late grandfather's twin,
a spinster given to plaids and "cosmic dance,"
who drank and smoked on the city edge of town
and spoke with an engaging huskiness
of conjunctions and ascendancies and drew
charts of the whole family, flaunting her
fragrant make-up, and her orangy hair
that she called "natural, the effect of time."
I was, of course, delighted when her house
burned down one night and she moved in with us—
January, a chimney fire they said.
So Aunt Louise settled into our spare room
making such gloomy forecasts that finally
my mother asked her to go easier—
although her readings usually came true.
Somebody on our road, she sighed, was doomed
at some point. Naturally I kept wondering.
I didn't relish leaving questions open.
I thought of a downcast home along our road.
Often that winter, on snowy Saturdays,
to see my mother's pallid smiling friend
who no longer had a husband (I forget why),
we'd trudge to this house of sooty icicles,
hot inside like an incinerator. Upstairs
her little daughter rested, not as old
as I was, sick, bedridden, who couldn't play
outside or go to kindergarten. I was told
she'd eaten paint from rungs of her iron bedstead
and twisted a bald point at the back of her head.
Once, while our mothers talked away, I stole

upstairs along the carpeted hall until, at the far
door's slit, I saw her. She was staring ahead.
A small, feathery blackbird beat in front of her eyes.
I didn't wave. A month later she was dead.
All day a powder snow broke through the cold.

Only a bracelet, yes, although for days
in the bank office, at intervals left alone,
I examined the piece, moving it round
and round the desktop, clasping, unclasping
its doubled-over, little slide-in snap,
until one snowy morning, tired of all
my pointless obsession with the thing,
calling it a casualty like the rest
of my life, I quietly dropped it into
a trash bin as I left the bank for lunch—
checking to see if Wade was anywhere.
He didn't mind the cold. I'd spotted him
all winter on various street corners, even
with snow falling. He seemed oblivious.
Sometimes he wore a hat. Or I'd catch him
loitering near a downtown restaurant
or shop—when I'd look out to see him
nonchalantly turn and stroll away.
After the divorce I had expected
him to disappear, his dirty work all done.
Or so I could assume his dirty work.
How else would Linda have cited actual
times, places, women, have learned enough
to hint at bank transactions she might like
to expose if I contested custody?
Yet when she left me and Wade didn't go,
but appeared sitting around unnaturally
often, I took occasion to rethink it.
This was early July, slowing my car
past the Carrenton during the rush hour,
without change of expression, I looked over.

There he was—drinking, of course. He seemed
to raise a glass to me as I passed him. That's
how bothered I was, by then, to think so, since
really his little gesture was ambiguous.
Home, I cooked a TV dinner and turned
the den lights up. I chalked my cue
and tried to shake it off. But I couldn't.
Had Linda ever hired him to begin with?
Could he be under hire still, if not
by Linda, then by someone else?
This may, in fact, have been the first evening
I really felt an inclination not
to do anything, forget the deals, forget
the womanizing (if you called it that), and simply
sequester myself in this low-timbered room
we'd annexed to the old colonial structure.
Just to relax. What was so dumb in that?
I should have said the table was antique,
bought from a big estate up north, the nap
heavy and the cushions dead until I did
them over, a richly dark mahogany frame
with mother-of-pearl diamonds, and the balls
ivory. Lit by those hanging overheads,
table and room looked nicely atmospheric
and told an eclectic story—mine: a buck's head
pinned to a sidewall (dull-eyed), a Winchester
over the window from my young days; snapshots
of boating with Linda and Bobby (as baby)
under the string of scoring beads; some chairs
and a maple table from my parents' farmhouse,
a contemporary swivel. And the glass doors
opened to my patio back area
lower than the front. I liked it.
                                                  No one,
because my yard sloped into several acres
of swampy undeveloped woodland, saw
me when I played.

                    Finally, after months,
my game was going more acceptably.
Earlier I had played a careless eight-ball,
or broken the rack and pocketed at random,
until this got so casual I devised
trickier set-ups, or I played nine-ball
to win—let's say—in not over two innings,
or tried to run the table in straight pool.
Serious stuff, you'd call it. And I studied
my manual, all the various terms
and photos and diagrams. Being self-taught,
it took a while to learn to freeze the head
and shoulders when I struck the cue-ball, left
knee bent and most of my weight forward.
And yet this evening everything got going.
My warm-up shots felt relatively smooth
and silky, I remembered to give each ball
its finishing caress. The clicks were good,
I liked the sound of them in the empty room,
in the open emptiness I'd felt lately.
Tonight, for once, I hit the cue-ball crisply,
finding my strategy right off. I took
an obvious move to give the nine a ride
and spread the cluster, while the eleven
rebounded softly into position zone.
That was simple enough to sink. From here
I sped the eleven down the rail to get
shape on the four, an easy rail-first carom
taking the twelve out, then a double kiss
sent several others rolling delightfully
to a workable three-ball combination,
the kind that makes it all worthwhile, my pace
unworried, easy, accelerating, the play
almost involuntary—not even keeping
a ball up for another round, but only
me there riding the wave until the last
ball dropped, without fudging, done, not over-
fancy, nothing for show, the perfect run.

How to continue? Is there a better way
than another?—as if you could ever know.
As if it mattered. That evening I poured
myself a scotch and water and sat back
in the swivel, flushed and empty-headed,
and while the elation settled, began to see
how long I'd taken learning the game well,
how many practices, until this sudden
run tonight, deserving (I thought) another
scotch and water. I sat again, enjoying
the slight disorientation of the drink,
and began to remember the way my own
father would fall into his big bones slowly
each morning, he wore sleep angels at the table.
"Anything good," he'd say, "happens more slowly
on earth than anyone wants it to," himself
born under the easy watery moon
of Cancer, as I, in fact, was meant to be
but came through late by three weeks and a day.
And he would tell us how everything burns,
slowly, of course, exactly as it has to,
it all burns, little stones at the wayside,
trees, grass, animals, even trivial
events flare into others coming our way,
with everything another kind of food.
  Wheel ruts, spokes of ice, puddles tightening, snow
   the night set down again lay county-wide,
our early-morning truck coughed breath into
the unbroken mystery of frozen air
and countless journey stops. Don't taste!
Cold iron fence will tear your tongue off.
Big garbage cans set out for us, with food
burning inside them, empty bottles, paper,
the mitten-soaking syrup juice that made
stains on the snow beside
porches of the intown winter rich

without hard farms to carry, hogs to feed,
their balconies facing Warren Avenue,
with names and numbers I had memorized,
and wondering, too, on their astrologies
(old lady Brandt who couldn't keep her tops on)
we came, we came. The dreamers had agreed
never to hear our feet breaking the crust—
although at times there simply seemed too much
garbage, I imagined the overspill
up with the planets, orbiting like planets,
calling, calling to be taken in.
How could it all get through that hole in the sky?
Crazy my innocence, my riding there
so much less helpful than I thought I was,
those Monday mornings, while I felt the lucky
touching signs we carried, my sign the Lion
that I wasn't yet, his sign the Crab,
the one I coveted, together climbing
sideways into God.
                        And there was also
in early days before the farm was sold
the unamusing little Farley Wilson, whose house
sat on a city sidestreet, who at school
seemed to be living under a spell, speaking
the right word only or not speaking,
twirling a forelock, telling me once, "I know
you're poor, you smell of apple tree wood."
I never liked him much, nobody could,
although his haughtiness vaguely intrigued me.
He claimed to own a cabinet of coins
at home, come down by family means,
with extra velvet bags all stashed away,
until, one summer afternoon, it happened
I stood beside his window case, his legs
straddled against me lightly, and how cool
a coin lay in my hand, his oldest

and most valuable, he said, this funny
lopsided thing, a wide-eyed little bird,
it was an owl: I felt the tuck and pull
of history, shadow and sunlight moving
on my hand at once, hints of old empires
that old Miss Weatherby told us about,
India, China, Greece, great merchant fleets
riding the wind-swept open sea since man
deserted Paradise and trade began. That night,
after my hours of intown visiting,
I woke up late somehow and, seeing the moon
faint on the window shade, got out of bed
and put my shade up very quietly
to see, perhaps, if the farm was really there.
And I saw trees, fields, haystacks. In the wan
moonlight, my father's garbage truck,
its bulbous wheel in back, looked like the obscene
squat of a pregnant cow under the elm tree.
A few fireflies floated right and left.
And along the shadowy, gravel path—oddly,
the animals long put up and the milking done—
hands in his pockets, came my father
walking slowly. He smiled; his hand shot out
in a wave. It was an awful scare for me.
Suddenly back in bed with the bedcovers
huddled up to my chin again—I laughed.

2

So I began a new routine of clearing
my mind entirely. I would not think of the past
again, I would not think of Wade, I would
not think of Wade sitting at the Carrenton
ordering drinks, while he read his newspaper
or looked around slightly or shifted positions,
as if he had all the useless time in the world.

I would not think of not thinking of him.
The summer stayed warm—warmer. Languid
afternoons held on, one after another,
I began easing an hour off my workday
to get home early while the light was good
for exercise and clearing out the junk wood,
limbs, overgrowth, dead brush accumulated
over so many summers of negligence.
My new routine: shower and swim. Enjoyable
to paddle backward slowly in the deep end,
to look up at a blue sky darkening, tree tops
and clouds, early evening clouds, shapes
steady or shifting as the wind moved them,
and let the whole year drop away, away.
The pool was there already when we'd bought
the house—a sunken, heated pool with a wide
runway of checkered tiles—we only added
the den to orient and open to it.
Swimming now I let the den's stereo
play out to cover the far-off traffic noise.
"That was the day also
when he interpreted her declining his little
gift of oak leaves on the walk as coolness."
Where did that come from, those words? What could
I be thinking? It was late July.
Nearly time again for Bobby's regular
end-of-the-month visit.
                          I cleaned his room
and set old toys out, placing them round
to affect naturalness, as if they expected him,
and also did my weekly kitchen clean-up.
He came by bus on Saturday. A tightrope
of little jokes, comments, wanderings
from room to room, getting the banter back,
his suitcase full of neatly folded outfits
I hadn't seen last month, pamphlets and magazines
like a traveling library tucked away.

We swam together in the pool, his body
small but supple for eight. At night he wanted
a story from his bookcase, calling me back
after I'd thought he was asleep, but it seemed
a vestigial, half-hearted wish. His eyes
no longer met mine when I checked, but finally,
turning his head, he gazed at the far window
as I read aloud the old words, trying
to give them tone, interest. . . .

> . . . Into the empty orchard dark
> Nils sailed, and so by moonlight
> He picked new peaches from the trees
> If they were ripe or not.
>
> When he had filled his basket floor
> He yanked a rope and soared
> Aloft again, to float at length
> Safely behind a cloud.
>
> By dawn he caught a favoring wind
> That gusted at his elbow,
> While faithfully some dark birds flew
> Above him or below.
>
> Wheat fields below him, too, and farms
> And cities and seacoast
> Rolled far away in muffled light
> To say goodbye at least.
>
> Now as the early morning sun
> Rose over a green sea
> He set his cruise-valve open, dozed,
> And drifted easterly.

So passed his idle hours away,
So passed his great balloon
High over seaclouds gathering
Toward afternoon.

He woke and wondered: Can I be
With luck the only one
Who never tried to sail his boat
Beyond the sun in vain?

He tossed pyrometer, compass out,
The dangling oars and anchor,
Even the champagne for his greeting
Party, every bottle.

Rustling sounds came from the sheet and blanket as
Bobby stirred, only to settle himself
better in the direction he already faced.

At this, the lightened-up balloon
Began to rise and rise,
To find the far belt of Orion
And the gentle Pleiades,

Where, farther in the dome-like quiet,
Stars of the Sisters play
Mindlessly into the Bull
Beyond the Milky Way

And, half asleep, the sidelong Crab,
Its center soft and fuzzy,
Floats with a flotsam radiance
As on the earliest day.

And so began his single journey
Angled to the Earth
And the unbounded Heavens,
Enjoying views of both.

I stopped. There were some pages left to go,
but I shut the book, since Bobby slept now,
giving in to his tiredness. So be it.
His sleeping profile looked a bit like Linda's.

3

The jump, the massé, my manual argues,
should be unnecessary, connoting rather
a flashiness or confession of poor planning,
just as the serious-minded novice learns
not to swagger, but cultivates a simple air
of command, knowing more than he uses,
a laid-back repertoire, just as the crack
gambler never talks much, only seems to,
so I played steadier once Bobby left,
compensatorily you may say, a midnight
and beyond midnight ritual, skid shot,
throw shot, deadball rolled to an angle,
off-hand running and reverse English,
follow and draw, the occasional thin
cut to the pocket, safeties, that became
quietly blooming seaflowers, like a life
hidden underwater. For nearly a week
a mild heatwave wouldn't dissipate.
The nights came moonless, hot, the air not
circulating, I left the glass doors open,
the screen being hit by fluttery bugs
trying to get in, the den lights throwing a soft
rectangle on the lawn.

             The fact
Wade never appeared outside the bank now
meant nothing. There was no need of it,
my earlier indiscretions over, no case
to investigate—in fact, a tidy smokescreen
of figures covered the old figures.
I was all right. Though something ruffled me,
something.... Why, despite my expectations,
did Bobby's visits disappoint me so,
only intensify the gap between us,
tenuous as his visits were, with Linda
able to drop them if they "proved unhealthy."
My moodiness returned. Only the games
alone at night, after a day's doldrums,
put me on the occasional upswing,
though paradoxically they made the next day
worse, burning me out. So now instead
of my anticipated week away
traveling upstate, what with its being
maybe too aimless a notion anyhow,
I returned the airline tickets and quietly
holed up in the house to reconnoiter.
Pleasant enough—just minor negatives.
I found it difficult to sleep at night,
my mind running to possible burglaries
throughout suburbia in vacation time,
ominous indications of the crime rate
rising, unruly teenagers on dope,
such craziness, and all the world's problems,
I should have wired the house up with alarms,
but hadn't.
          Saturday, anyhow, I ventured
out by foot. A handsome two-mile trek
down to the city, unusual for me
to be hiking out so far unnecessarily—
having developed, too, a summer cold,
the kind that saves itself for your vacation,

but the day was a sunny, refreshing one,
with a light morning breeze, and furthermore
it felt better not to have the car seen
but, rather, just to wander by and appear
to be sitting down as the whim struck me.
I arrived and took an outdoor table vacated
by a mother and squabbling children—fine, at least,
to escape that sort of thing myself—the waiter
swept fries and shredded napkins into a dustpan,
smoothed the oilcloth, and I gave my order
of a sandwich and looked round the busy place—
casually. My heart leapt. Wade wasn't there.
After all that! A healthy crowd, though. Twenty
odd tables filled to near capacity.
Then I saw him at a small one under
the awning, set back rather passively, by
the hotel window where the gold characters
CARRENTON and the day's menu floated.
Reading some magazine, he sat half-turned
away from me, and looking studious.
He wore an irritating small beret
(as if the shade under the awning made
it cooler there), a gray shirt, open-collared,
legs crossed and partly hidden by the oilcloth.
Past other tables and the uneven breaks
between waiters and moving customers, I saw
a glass of red wine set in front of him
with empty saucers to one side, the place's
way of calculating the bill here, maybe;
but what an hour to begin drinking! He looked
sallow, wrinkled, sunken below the cheekbones,
not sad, not happy—not anything, really.
Somehow I wanted to beat the shit out of him.
His eyes stayed lowered to whatever magazine
intrigued him so. He appeared to have lost weight.
Suddenly I realized he was sitting
a certain way—aimed in my usual

direction from the bank, perhaps to allow
quick glances, his old system of trying
to see me while pretending not to see me,
knowing I'd seen him, pretending not to know.
If so, he was handling it stylishly.
Quite in keeping with the service here, your basic
reason for the noontime turnover, everything
chic and stylish down to the sandwiches.
When my chicken club arrived I ate it slowly,
delaying, also, over the sprouts and side
cucumber wedges, to see what might occur.
But now, on a mid-day outing, I was spotted
by two old ladies I'd helped once with investments.

"Good afternoon there!" came the inevitable waves
and some laughter from them. "You're looking well."
"You look well, too," I said back to them. "Are you?"
"Yes, we are, thank you!"
                              Irrationally
their presence put me at a disadvantage;
and uneasy in my plan to stretch the last
inconspicuous bites out, and not wanting coffee,
I paid the waiter and left. For me, of course,
there was time to dawdle—the whole week, if need be.
So I took a movie in, and wandered back
afterward. I didn't really care
if he was there or not. But he wasn't.
Premature for the supper crowd, no more
than a handful of couples at scattered tables.
I had a rye and water, waiting. Darkness
began to hover. I ate a small meal.
Perhaps I should have walked to his hotel
right then. Perhaps I should have finally sought
him out, once and for all, talked, satisfied
my wondering. (Last spring, of course,
after I'd traced him to an old brownstone,
half-modernized hotel, and slipped the doorman

twenty, I had learned something: name of Wade,
hanging around here several years and running
a slow detective agency upstairs
to judge by the few visitors. "People
don't need your private eye these days," he'd added.
Well, no . . . I checked the mailbox: H. Charles Wade,
confirmed him later in the yellow pages
open to 7-day, 24-hour business.
He must have been delighted to catch Linda's.)

I had a few more whiskeys. Still no show.
I felt tired. Took a taxi home. Dark, a bit
misty, though I spotted immediately
the raccoon damage, finding I'd left the garage
doors up and den lights going by mistake.
Stupidly I'd left the cellar light on.
Raccoons, woodchucks—often I'd pick them off
leaving the woods, damned scavengers. Tonight, though,
pleasantly tipsy, I left the mess for later,
hardly hoped to play a passable game
but did, the cue-ball zippy and obedient.
Even before vacation I'd begun
going to bed later and later, learning
to anticipate the dawn light. Only once
did I get thrown off—suddenly near dawn
a quiet rain, obscuring the usual
shifts of sky, and always suddenly
rain again would make me think of Linda,
feelings of loss I didn't worry over
most of the time—and now vacation had me
lunching for breakfast at the Carrenton,
coffee and eggs by noon, parking sensibly
short of the café, as to maintain
my casual approach by foot. But Wade
had taken off. That was Sunday, I remember.
I strolled until the first movies opened,
also checking at intervals all Monday,

and took my evening meal there, but no Wade.
Why not? Funny what dark considerations
can bubble up at times like these. Could he
be spying on me by some counter-strategy,
manipulating my behavior, laughing—
intolerable, making a fool of me!
Or could he be a so-called "open shadow"
meant to be spotted? . . .
My sudden fury passed. I felt better.
And Tuesday he returned, as ever, the heatwave
broken finally, sky overcast. A late
evening clientele, more dressy than noon's,
gathered inside, though Wade and I and maybe
a dozen others took the open air.
Why not enjoy the pleasant summer air?
Clear weather, and some little banners out.
He must have noticed me arrive. His shoulders
appeared hunched, something newly, oddly
frail about him. Or mere self-consciousness?
Sporting his tweed beret again, he sat
relaxing into wine and cheese, no entree.
This was becoming a repetitious story,
mundane, with finely tuned variations.
Still, I have to admit my mild respect—
how he projected a certain artistry
beyond me, even in these to-and-fro
wanderings from the café. Again tonight
not even a brief glance over: his clear
avoidance of me had grown vaguely humorous.
Actually, with the break from my work schedule,
I'd felt a partial fondness springing up
for him: maybe I'd rather overstressed
his deviousness, his purposes, he might
indeed be lonely, wanting sympathy, having
no friends or family or cronies, nothing
to keep him going really. But money?
You couldn't call the café inexpensive.

What about his floundering business? Did he
have outside funds, benefactor, private
income—who knew what to say about this?

Nothing arrived to mark the end of summer,
wanderers passed the café, often with dogs,
and faint warm breezes came down those nights
to ruffle the small leaves of trees growing
out of the pebbled circles, with their Romanesque
repeating wire loops, prettier than tin
sleeves or stick supports. Waiting for him
I spent a long time studying those trees,
watching and studying the leaves that curled
partly and turned by the breeze, shimmered,
I took an interest in details that could
both cover and manifest a mystery,
as if the very leaves themselves hoped to be caught
up swirling around some single, inexpressible
silent word. This may sound foolish, unclear,
it does to me, actually. Street music
returned, a nightly itinerant group
(one of the mayor's rejuvenation plans)
played fiddle, accordion, and tambourine,
I heard their pretty music drifting round
a corner, a tune I'd heard before somewhere,
something like

and I found tears welling in my eyes,
not painfully. I felt nearly at peace.
It was like memory, a return of beauty
floating not just ahead of me, but behind me,
a confirmation of all I had come from.

You know how one indulges, whimsically,
a silly fling one later can't slip out of,
well, here I was, guessing that although
I couldn't control his chance arrivals, surely
with patience I could make him *leave* before me,
I arrived on Wednesday, quite a humid night,
determined to outsit and follow him
and play the shadower he preferred to be.
Not much of a wind was moving, like the day
before, to rustle the awning or cool anyone,
but it didn't bother you if you stayed still.
Wade was already comfortable. He wore
a buttoned madras jacket in cream colors
and looked as if he could be heading somewhere.
Wade, almost elegant! Well, yes. I chose
a table closer than he might have liked,
and rattled the big menu gently. Ordered a few
aperitifs. Then snails. Then tournedos,
a tossed salad. Cheese plate. Yes, I could
dawdle here as elegantly as he could.
Chablis: I nursed a half-bottle through the
seven-to-eight hour. A little sweat
settled on the oilcloth, on my forehead.
My wine went tepid. And predictably
Wade kept sipping, ordering separate glassfuls
as if he knew the preferred system, reading
his fool magazine again, or a new one.
Customers thinned out. Or intermingled
with the happier after-theatre set for drinks
only, and these eased away. It got late,
more obvious we were the two steadies,
more obvious this waiting-the-other-out
routine could fritter on forever, given
our stubborn set of mind. Then as he shifted
fractionally in the café light and shadow
letting his jacket, already a loose-fitter,
fall open slightly, there was a gun. A second

before his elbow settled again, I caught
the gun-bulge and a black protruding handle.
"You, sir, would you—"
                    "No," I said. "No. Nothing.
The check, please." For my idea came—quickly.
This was the smartest thing I ever did,
I kept telling myself, having paid and walked
away—now heading straight to his hotel,
down through the old quarters; the smartest thing.

4

Nobody stopped me at the elevator.
I rode it to the seventh. Quickly I found
701, his door, at the overlit end
of a corridor, folded newspaper waiting.
He'd got his name displayed, also a doormat,
but I didn't hang around. Downstairs and going
outside again, I counted up: his shade
half-drawn, no light. All this was gaining
a jaunty excitement to it. Across and facing
opposite, stood two turn-of-the-century
flophouses, the dingier one closer, but never
mind, I crossed and entered the lobby
where a whiskery night clerk sat half-dozing,
an old head on his hand, dozens of keys
like little tongues in the mail cubbies behind him.
Not a very popular hotel—or
everybody was out, let's say. He muttered
something to my "Single, facing the street?"
How uncommunicative these people are,
so taxed by non-responsibility.
And the elevator, too, in these places
is never on the ground floor waiting, but makes
jackhammer clanks as it grinds slowly down.
I took a slow trip up (reading FLORIDA

ONLY A JUMP AWAY, along with various
graffiti, *See Marie in 33,*
and *Have a good time in 69* below it,
as if some local mucker thought it rhymed).
Another consideration: why is the room
they give you always so far from the elevator,
a couple of turns at least? Already I saw
my room before I got there: a low bureau
and chair, dust balls, rigidly sagging mattress,
not that I bothered to turn the standing lamp on,
but sat, with neon flickering in, and looked
out on Wade's hotel and small businesses,
drugstore, pinball, adult novelties, some broken
signs, discounts. I sat there several hours,
sorry for Wade, sorry he had to live
in such circumstances, sorry he didn't arrive
more quickly, and once I dropped off even,
and woke, the street empty. It was darker,
everybody gone home. Then I saw him
rounding the corner by the pizzeria,
shuffling somewhat. He must have had a skinful
in him by now, although he looked unduly
chipper for the hour, as he ambled closer,
gazing downward, oblivious, straight
into his hotel.
                With a gambler's instinct
I counted to a leisurely one hundred,
hitting the mark exactly—his light went on!
At this he appeared brisk and business-like
(all but his head, cut by the window shade)
and plainly, in full view, shifted the gun
to his top bureau drawer, a careless gesture,
I thought, since anyone like me could see it.
And he moved out of sight. Another dull
period. Finally he returned in pajamas
and, leaning forward, pulled his shade entirely.
A faint light on the window shade went out. I lay

exhausted, trying to sleep now, for I'd want
to catch his morning exit (and could hardly
expect the desk downstairs to ring me up),
I tried to relax, and later heard the faraway
traffic fade, and heard someone rummage
into the room a few doors down, retching.
A classy hangout. I ought to come more often.

I woke up, sunlight striking the bed.
                                           His window
shade was up, no motion evident.
Groggy and not especially happy at having
missed a beat, I made for the Carrenton.
When Wade failed to materialize after coffee
and eggs, I walked around a bit, and caught
the last decent film opening at noon,
having seen everything now except the skins,
and strolled again, periodically spot-checking
the café and Wade's window.
                                           Before night, though,
finally irked at this fancy runaround
he was giving me at all times of day,
I bought binoculars, a Little Ben
alarm clock, a hip flask of Early Times,
and headed back, late, idly through the less
savory sections. The little whores were out,
street-loitering runaways in tanktops, a few
inside at counters, talking or looking out,
tougher and younger than ever. I nearly began
to wonder what a quick pick-up might be like
for somebody like me who's never really
fantasized about them—what casual,
what dirty hands they must have, and how would
they talk to you, what sort of wetnesses,
smells? —Crazy, crazy, I was losing touch.

I took another stint watching his window.
(Having overlooked toothbrush and razor,
I had a slightly disheveled and bristly feeling.)
Nobody much wandered the streets. Why did
my heart jump at the sight of anyone
turning the corner—even a dog once? Whiskey
and water, no ice: a prolonged vigil
whose first part ended with the flask half empty.
Abruptly his light went on. Binoculars!
I hadn't noticed anything at all.
A thrill ran up my spine to see him finally
at midnight stand beside his desk (his shirt
showing thin arms, not muscular, maybe once
had been strong, only a slackness now) and sit
down, open a drawer, bring out a notebook
and begin writing. Slowly. Sometimes he'd flick
a few pages back, or gaze up pausing,
thumb against chin, or flick his underlip
or rub the inside neck of his t-shirt.
After a while he tore a page out, crumpled it,
tossing it sideways. Then more pages. Others.
He proceeded to work himself into a fever,
almost feverish, feverish for him.
A hubbub of crumpled papers. What was he doing?
What (for that matter, really) was I doing
myself here, crouching, sweaty, my heart
pounding, elbows on windowsill, glued to
these poor ridiculous tools of espionage—
me, my life falling to shambles, yes
to shambles around me, to nothing, how absurd,
how stupid this whole search was, even if Wade
indeed had ever been Linda's informer, or knew
my weaknesses by heart, or hated me,
how absurd, I saw, to have thought any secret
gathering of details could clarify it.
Look at these hands. Look. Trembling! My arms
trembling. What was the matter? Was it

too late to forget all this? to leave? Too late
to understand? Why didn't he look up?
I had been watching in darkness a long time.
Now putting aside binoculars (which hardly
helped anyway) I turned the floor lamp on,
but Wade, as chance would have it, shut his notebook,
turned his light off and left the desk area,
only a faint interior glow staying
inside awhile, until that, too, went out.

It was the next evening—yes, late Friday,
it had to be, considering, counting back—
we sat six tables apart.
                         (Not bothering
to shadow him earlier, I'd driven home
for a quick shower and shave, was starting a game,
having, apparently in my late-night stupor,
left the table uncovered and balls scattered,
when the phone rang, Connolly at the office,
seen me strolling around. Where were the papers?
He sounded openly abrupt. Our client
was "justifiably pissed," negotiations must
follow in person, vacation or not. I lined up
airplane tickets for Saturday, located
the papers in my briefcase, reviewed them
over supper at home before a drive downtown.)

We sat, to repeat myself, six tables apart.
Wade's fare tonight was brandy in a snifter.
For me "vin ordinaire" was good enough.
After a while, of course, he took another
glass, as I myself did; after a decent
time we had another round. Whenever
he gestured for the waiter, I did too,
although my weaker drinks gave me the advantage.
Soon we were into half a dozen slow ones.
Customers came and went. It didn't matter.

Beyond midnight there was just our young waiter
leaning lackadaisically in the doorway
riding it out with two last customers.
Morning haze had softened the café lights.
An unblinkable glow to objects, everything.
Noise of the city faded, mostly. I heard
a far-off whirr of crickets—or was it
my dizziness and fatigue?—as Wade, no other
gesture open to him finally, turned to me
and seemed to smile.
                        I left immediately.
All the same, early next morning
before my business trip, I dropped a letter
off at his hotel, Fairfax 701,
inviting him home on Sunday (I'd be returning
around suppertime, so come at seven or eight).
I kept the tone discreetly casual,
not overfriendly, to avoid awkwardness
if I had missed the mark completely—ending it:

>   Could we enjoy chatting together?
>   Take the footpath around the house
>   to the back. Let's have a drink or two.

Then what a peacefulness came over me.
A day later, home from Cincinnati,
I unpacked, relaxed, dawdled over some
nine-ball in the den, an unhurried game.

It had rained lightly. A brief rain, leaving
the backyard trees and lawn fresh-smelling,
the tiles shiny. I felt a warmth, a sense
of connections I hadn't felt since early childhood.
Funny. As I'd expected, footsteps sounded
behind the house, a rustling, just past seven,
as he walked slowly up the steps to my terrace
wearing his summer jacket, with an umbrella,

his face typically calm and toneless.
He slipped on the tiles slightly—recovered himself,
and blinked without much change of expression.
As I watched him approaching along the poolside
a fierce new liquid started, sprouted from
my gums, or under my tongue, a greenish
acrid taste. His steps were tentative.
I pushed a chair to the back doorway to pull
my shotgun down. I aimed and fired the first barrel
and struck him, high. If he wore his gun on him
he didn't reach, but under the jolt swung out,
pivoting halfway around, his hand
to one shoulder, his back to me. The second
shot must have split his spine, for he doubled back
into the water, sharply crashing, toppling head down,
ripples, then smoky red, a slow blending I
knew even then was inexplicable.
Somewhere, nowhere, a far scream began
that might have been either of ours, but wasn't,
the sound continuing through roots and swamp
even as I dragged him into the woods
and got my shovel—maybe his gun fell out
along the way, I never found it—continuing
until I drained the pool of him, and filled
it up again, and slept, and drove to work.

THE SHADE TREES
(Narrator: Wade's brother-in-law)

My various friends call me humorous,
sentimental, and a few other things.
I say I'm realistic down to the toes.
Business had taken me to the States
that September, not friendship, but I saw
no reason not to see Wade,
my initial stopover being his city,
and Margaret also, traveling with me
to visit relatives and the old turf,
favored it. Many years earlier Wade,
after his wife's—my sister's—death,
had been so generous in sending us
some of her oils and watercolors
I'd kept a perennial spot for him. Who couldn't
enjoy his wry, rather witty asides
on most subjects, his twists of mind?
For a while we corresponded. It dropped
to a random holiday card. My recent letters
detailing our arrival went unanswered.
This piqued the practical side of me.

My phone call (on arrival) to Wade's hotel
determined he'd disappeared, his rent
unpaid and mail accumulating.
Already, as the naïvely turned-up relative
on my end of the line, I could feel myself
being tagged for money, though I agreed
to stop over, if briefly, the next morning,
with time enough before delivering
my talk on medicine and computers.
How dusty it was! But a serviceable
apartment, with a brightly updated
kitchenette-sitting nook in the condensed
style of those days, the walls displaying
some paintings. While the hotel manager
(taking my presence for dispensation?)
jimmied the lock to Wade's file cabinet,

I examined the rather more obvious letters
in a wooden box on his dresser, tied
by a frayed ribbon, among clips and elastics.
Edges had faded. It was small blue paper.
In an odd, familiar dazzle I recognized
my sister's handwriting floating up at me,
letters kept without envelopes, apparently
in order, though undated, without return
address—ah yes, my sister's usual
nonchalance. I read the top few.

    Dear Mr. Wade,
        I would like to stress
    my thanks again with this last payment.
    Although it may be years before
    my life regains equilibrium,
    your help made such a difference.
    Kindly accept this small bonus
    as token—and with it, thanks.
        Sincerely,
        C. deRochemont

    Dear Mr. Wade,
        You were most kind
    to return the check, although I am
    choosing to send it back again.
    Yes, I realize you are "all right."
    But remember, too, my late husband
    left me comfortably well off.
    It really gives me pleasure to
    extend the favor. Accept it please.
        My appreciation,
        C. deRochemont

Dear Mr. Wade,
     Your last letter finds me,
after these many weeks, in England
visiting my brother and his family.
Forwarding was slow. I apologize
for any delay in answering you.
However, this reappearance of
my check somewhat distresses me.
Because most of the money was yours
by salary, and only part of it
a bonus, I hope we can settle up
with this adjusted figure, and
when I return to the States, you might
allow me to do *something* for you.
     With (final) thanks,
     Catherine deRochemont

When she returned to the States? We'd thought
my sister would never leave! She joined us
there in Hampstead after the illness
and death of her first husband, a brilliant
irritable architect I never liked
as much as—later—I liked Wade.
But suddenly she was alone, and since
Margaret especially felt sympathy,
inviting her over seemed the obvious
gesture. It was a bad time for Carrie,
who recuperated slowly, almost too slowly
I tended to feel; she painted, worked
in a store downtown, and helped us, taking
care of the children when Margaret's
career and pregnancy grew difficult,
and began, it seemed, a correspondence
which now, I admit, like a voyeur
I scanned with vague curiosity.

Dear Mr. Wade,
    What a surprise, how entertaining
to hear from you. Just a few letters
are coming to me from the States,
not many. Finally my present life
is taking on more reality than
the past.
    This family is a pleasure!
I act as a kind of "au pair" girl
(twenty years overage, no doubt)
to the children, Fred and Vanessa,
who are nine and seven. Fred performs
clever chemistry experiments from a kit
with his father, the two of them showing
an amusing rivalry over chemicals,
something I can see taking other
forms later, while Vanessa studies dance,
and is thinking also of the violin.
She has a graceful agility with music
(as I did once, somewhat), a sweet
imitative flair. She could be an actress.
    In many ways, it's good seeing
another country. Have you enjoyed
traveling abroad yourself? Sometimes
I feel very superfluous, though,
especially in my lonelier moments,
despite the help Gerald says I am.
He's kind, my brother, and you are also
kind to remember an old client so.
    Best wishes,
    Catherine deRochemont

Dear Mr. Wade,
    What a fine letter!
I hardly expected, when I idly
asked about traveling, so detailed

a picture of your Italian childhood.
Your memory is quite remarkable.
How good that your father taught history
those many years in Florence. Few children
have the experience of two cultures.
 I know how William, with his
architect's eye, would have enjoyed
the Hampstead landscape. Our town
itself is built like a fishing village
without the sea, houses set on
the brow of a hill, and steps running
down through little gaps and alleyways
to Heath Street, where High Street goes on
downhill, four miles, in changing names
to London.
 These many Hampstead names
are delightful. I've taken to strolling
on mornings along Well Walk, or down
Flask Walk, Frognal Lane, Church Row,
to Holly Hill, visiting the intown
booksellers, chatting with people
at the very top of Heath Street
by Whitestone Pond. Despite our changing
world there is still a peculiar ease
to these well-kept Georgian houses
of our section, the graveyard
just inside Church Row, and the confident
Sunday bells. Uproad, our Heath
is a wonderful, wandering, untamed area
good for walks and painting.
 And I've been painting and reading
a lot lately—rummaging through
the fine old leather volumes
Gerald inherited from our father,
a library he's quite proud of, although
he doesn't read much lately. Jane Austen's
novels are what I'm doing now.

    I enjoyed your letter—very good
everything goes as usual.
    Cordially, and good wishes,
    Catherine

Peculiar to hear these vague, these slightly
off-putting echoes, my family analyzed,
my home and library thumb-nailed, thirty
years later, this September morning
(and all those memories of the old
house in Hampstead, before we'd found it
more sensible to live in London).
What was she doing into my Jane Austen?
Curious, too, how well she'd foreseen
traits and tendencies that took years
to surface clearly so I could see them.
It wasn't difficult to begin
riffling through for news of myself.
Frankly, at this, I felt the old sibling
jealousy rising up again, still
Carrie the older sister, talented,
somehow protected by her dark beauty,
she could do anything, ways naturally
opening up for all her adventures
and eccentricities—I remembered, in childhood,
an umbrella dance she took through the house
from chairbacks to floor, sofa and stairs,
ourselves detained and waiting to give her
smiles and applause, and how I thought—
she will always float through life like this,
beautiful, easy. And I will be myself.
And I wondered, will I ever be drained
of bitterness?
    But continuing here,
while the impatient manager rattled away,
I read more quickly, catching extracts
on larger paper now.

Dear Chuck,

No, I don't mind your writing. In fact, I welcome this correspondence, if you won't expect miracles of me. And certainly please do send me that autobiography you're doing.

Thanks for your concern over my moods, which are better, now that I'm painting each day. I work afternoons, as well, in a small second-hand bookstore down in Hampstead, run by a very good-natured bachelor, in his mid-forties I'd say. I find it a diversion being around customers and the neatly arranged shelves and tables of old books. He isn't the way he sounds, he's quietly lecherous actually, in a gentlemanly, suppressed English way. He toured me around Keats's house, and a few nights ago we strolled again in the lovely, sedate Keats Grove, and I thought of that young man snuffed out so early, and his bravery. None of your tree-haunting nightingales this year, though. I can't remember what nightingales sound like, but there weren't any.

I keep thinking how the dead and dying must envy us—us, the living—how William certainly did, dying. Something was lost in the end, in his anger and pain. But I keep telling myself that the end itself doesn't matter, what matters is how we live every day. Too easily we forget what we hold in our hands, forget how the saddest thing is simply to be gone.

What cases, by the way, are you tackling these days? Anything startling? You never mention them, although I realize they may, of course, require secrecy.

Best wishes,
Catherine

. . . Bradley (my bookstore pal) has become more intimate lately. Rather a relief, since a real affection for me seemed to be lurking in the shadows. I've met his father now,
his mother died ten years ago.

At our Hampstead cinema, which specializes in revival, we saw Cocteau's "Orpheus," a rather strung-out and compulsive sort of movie, finally too effete, too period-piece for me, obsessed with style. Bradley thought so too. There was a display of some local artists in the lobby, and it struck me I could also show there, if I stay in England awhile, or move here permanently.

. . . Bradley and I took a picnic lunch last Sunday to the Heath, ten minutes' walk up from Redington Road. It's truly a delightful place, with the hawthorne and late fall flowers nestled in, the paths, sudden views of Kent and Surrey to the south. What stays with me, though, is the sounds of those trees, like a kind of spirit blowing, as Bradley said, waiting there even in the quietest weather. Have you ever wanted to create something so beautiful that people would say it was there already, you simply found it for us? . . .

*

No, I won't keep dwelling on Bradley et al. Thanks for your latest autobiographical section. It's getting quite long! The passages on the robberies and the archeological digs are especially effective. My only criticism is that there's so little of yourself in it. And the tone—isn't it, at its weakest, a little too wise-cracking? Sometimes it's hard to believe or understand the actual things you're reporting, or at least to realize your connection with them. After all, aren't you the real subject? Couldn't you explain your emotions about these people and places, letting us know what you're feeling at the time?

*

. . . of this third-floor studio my brother fixed up for me, its windows overlooking our courtyard of grass and bushes, some scattered flagstone, a fine pair of cedars at the west edge. Today there's an inch of snow on them! Gone soon, no doubt. There seem to be fewer swallows and swifts doing their arcs in the sky. I'm painting more freely and quickly from this window, a series now, I'm trying to capture, at these different times, our downhill silhouette of rooftops, so haunting in the afternoon light, especially when the angles begin to shift—catching the gray shingles, chimney-pots, leaving the courtyard down below. Sometimes I think I'm trying to find the perfect moment here that sums everything up, brings it together, some perfect moment you'll always remember and build on later. If such a thing exists? This courtyard, when you're down there, it feels so spacious and elegant, but later it's a boxed-in little area, looking so arbitrary from up here, like a toy. And at dusk, these sharpening edges of roofs, always diminishing, and the fading sunlight....

*

... But I like your distinction—wherever you get it—between the hedgehog and the fox. Possibly I *am* more like the hedgehog, wanting a single answer, and you are the fox, wanting many. I hope I don't *look* very much like a hedgehog, though. Whereas you do, I think, look rather like a fox at times....

*

... these amusing little dichotomies you keep tossing out to me. I don't know what to make of them. But our cheerfulness cheers me, anyway. I see you wandering the streets, watching the whole spectacle, watching yourself in it, and the puzzles around you, and yourself always humorous and secretive, a bit cynical, perhaps needing a little warmth you don't like to admit. Not that I understand you—I realize by now I'll never quite understand you. But how can you really maintain that reality is just on the surface? You say you're not looking for "clues" to anything hidden behind actions, only trying to see exactly what those actions are. Well, I can't agree with you that life is all surface, with nothing—to use your vocabulary—but these so-called questions of "fact" and questions of " relationship." Where did you pick up this funny idea, Chuck? As you know, I believe in delving to the deeper mystery. After all, you haven't explained why these "facts," as you put it, exist to begin with. Something that goes beyond these dichotomies. On these deeper questions, doesn't your philosophy lead you, finally, to a position of silence? ... But I suppose you won't answer that, to be amusing.

(They went on, these letters, possibly
a dozen more of them, discussing theatre,
museum exhibitions, books and philosophy,
her side trips to Canterbury and the Cotswolds,
becoming warmer and signed variously
"my best," "as ever," "with affection,"
although the tenor and thrust of the discussion
began to rankle me slightly. Why
was I left out? It was my house,
you'd expect to be mentioned more than
tangentially, I thought—and skimmed for my name.)

    ... Truly, my apologies for letting your letters pile up. I haven't forgotten, I was tired—no, tired isn't the answer. When nothing arrived from you these two weeks—and I certainly don't blame you for it—I began to worry, and I'm still worrying. Are you ill, or injured, are you insulted? I realize now that I've been avoiding my end of the correspondence out of fear, a simple fear of becoming too close to you, to anyone, so soon after William's death. I may be wrong to say this. But your friendship matters greatly to me, you must know that.

    Anyway, spring is here. Today I'm testing a new hammock Gerald has hung for me in the courtyard—he is constantly kind and thoughtful. Though actually I prefer the yard chairs. This is a warm April, very little rain. The activity all over town is picking up. Gerald's away again—another medical convention. He's doing so well, someday he may be famous. The bushes and gardens along Redington Road are flowering finally, making a pleasant walk downtown each morning. I have quit the bookstore. . . .

*

. . . Thank you for your letter.
Last night a strange thing happened—I walked in my sleep. I had got downstairs without falling or upsetting anything, half-dreaming that I was backstage at some outdoor amphitheatre, when finally I wrenched myself awake by rattling the latch of the French doors going into the courtyard. (They wouldn't open.) I stood there dazed, with a little light coming through the windows and lace curtains into the living room. The long Georgian living room. I saw the familiar things, settee and chairs and piano, but I still believed, for a few moments, I was somewhere else. I crept upstairs like a thief!
All day today I haven't been able to shake the experience. To escape the mood, I walked up to the Heath and tried some sketching (poorly). But I felt happier than usual. There was a warmth in the air all around me, everything seemed to be floating away—the drawing, my body, my whole visit to Hampstead. It was like a signal of some kind that I ought to be leaving England, leaving Gerald and this family who have been so perfect to me. I will always love them for that. But I need to be putting it behind me, leaving it behind. . . .

Well, yes, she had left us behind,
back there, somewhere . . . a warmth, sunlight, a more
innocent time maybe? But the manager
was shuffling Wade's papers now, easily
covering the whole kitchen table with them,
and I, with that uneventful packet
of Carrie's letters in my hand,
I saw that I'd actually been expecting
some revelation (now that I'd found none)

and how, for all my curiosity, I was
left with that pointless embarrassment
you sometimes feel when you enter a room
talking, only to find the room empty;
and while I stood there, foolish, not yet
realizing I would keep these letters
as a small legacy of emotion,
as something, anyhow, left over,
all I could hear was the obviously
charitable voice of my sister, a sister
I'd never especially loved, speaking
at the outset of thirty years, before
her successful marriage to Wade, her death,
and now (as I hadn't guessed that morning)
Wade's final disappearance. Two more
on the original notepaper:

        ... of all
our questionings. And now
I see why you returned my check
five months ago. You meant to continue
the conversation, didn't you?
You knew from the beginning.

        But, Chuck, I ask you
to reconsider. Or else, perhaps,
to ask me again, much later, knowing
this: I never can have children.
A miscarriage settled that years ago.
There was no reason to speak
of it earlier. But you deserve
a family, should have one.
        And how, really, could we
ever be suited? From what little
we know of each other we're opposites,
with different pasts and presents,
attitudes, needs, philosophies,

we'd be forever arguing,
and I am older than you—in fact,
whatever would an odd child of ours
have been like? It's interesting
to speculate.
       I admit to longings
over these months I haven't described,
perhaps out of loneliness,
but if you asked me over again,
I'm not sure how I'd answer
even then.

            *

       Yes, I will come home.

       I almost think this will be
my last letter to you. I feel happy.
Can one be entirely happy and still
be writing letters about it?
Is that why some great people
in history have written nothing?

       There's a light breeze now,
the sun is making funny patterns
on Gerald's terrace, or rather
the leaves are, or both.

       Somebody next door has just gone
inside to make tea. I hear a whistle.
People are strolling downhill, I hear
laughter beyond the wall and these trees.
Someday I will look back and say, that day
was magic for me. But very ordinary.
I mustn't forget this. You must try
not to forget this. Under the
shade trees I have made my mind.

from
THE RING ROAD (A SEQUENCE)

for Nancy

Only a single, soft
cloud appeared in the sky
the day that you were born.
They say all afternoon
it hung aloft,

an anomaly in the blue
and almost windless weather,
finally settling vaguely
westward and overhead.
It liked the view

(that long ago July)
of farms and drumlin hills
and country roads, the white,
black-shuttered family homestead.
A single cloud in the sky.

I

Before my brother was born
I sat on a kitchen chair
and looked through dangling legs
to where the linoleum squares
made an obscure design.

Before my brother was born
I saw how the kitchen tiles,
right-angled or upside down
to look various, were really
identical. This is one

of my first memories.
Another is my mother
lurching from bed, then gone
away from us—to bring back
a baby who whimpers and cries.

*

In summer the fireflies
come from the meadow up,
blinking from where they all
began?—and yet my brother
and I think otherwise:

They have huddled in our trees
and gradually grown
restive and cool and eager
to give back the moonlight,
becoming fireflies

to float in total ease,
although we can't explain
the occasional shortfall
before they come again,
touching our busy days.

So many gods pour out
of the sky on autumn nights,
pounding and flashing, the placid
prints my mother has hung
in the hall seem incomplete.

A child ogles the sunrise
in one print. In another
he holds a conch to his ear.
Next he tastes a strawberry.
Now he presses his nose

to some flower on a trellis.
Then strokes a fluffy rabbit. . . .
So go the sensible gods.
But there are more than five
gods, these evenings tell us.

*

The goblins underneath
our house want it their way,
tunneled and wayward, many
with hatchets and mallets they
chuckle under their breath.

Some casual remark
brought forth the hard-working goblins.
No moonbeams ever reach
the cellar, where on a full moon
I hear them chipping rock.

The world I would replace
tonight won't go away.
It's here to stay. It is
deeper than you, than I am,
deeper than any of us.

White snow against the red
berries, or the other way
around: I was a little
tyke at the time, grade school
at the end of the road.

Miss Miller hated the snow,
she spoke of that fact, and how
she hated "things in bloom,"
checking us into home room.
She had nowhere to go.

One day she drank the red
wine from her cupboard, I'm told.
I do not think it was wine,
it was too hot, too cold
at the end of the road.

*

Music is still a mystery
like the stars and planets.
Many who write of music
tell us largely about
its being far away

or suddenly overheard,
as if it were not here—
as if we could ignore
either its harmony or
destruction. But when he untied

his little boat, leaving
willow and bank, and rowed
out onto the dark lake
below high cliffs he felt life's
mathematical breathing.

If holiday turkey is sliced
extremely thin it doesn't
necessarily taste
any better. If antique
ladderback chairs are placed

close to facilitate
adult conversation and the
circulation of Mary
it doesn't necessarily
help you to sit up straight.

Everything we're able
to say about family starts
with food: the kind of food,
the amount, the server,
the seats assigned at the table.

*

Her toe on the carpet. A buzz,
and almost instantly
Hannon appears, to clear
dessert, and everything is
exactly as it was

except for dirty napkins
and a spot on the tablecloth
where my blueberry pie had been.
Never can I escape it!
I hate the way my sins

are uncovered, one by one,
and registered by those
who glance away—my sins
uncovered one by one
and not remarked upon.

Leaving his family, a child
walks through an alley courtyard
where ashcans tilt. Grass tufts
skewer the mildewed brick.
Although he smells a mild

piss, it's refreshing because
the standards are not high here.
Someone has left the gate open.
Nobody cares or knows much
what anyone says or does.

So it's pleasant to be
passing servanted homes
unseen—only myself
spotting the weeds and dog-poop
and swill of a week's debris.

*

They said a stranger hid
and leapt from trees. "Springtime!"
one of the jock-boys joked,
who hadn't seen him.
None of us had.

April already, bush
and crocus in bloom, night rains
washing the riverbank
and lifting the wide river.
Some of the girls were hushed

or giggling. "He shows his tool!"
And did the night rains wash
him, too? What beauty or blood
or danger swelled the Charles
I walked along to school?

The world is off, and we
don't know the tilt of Heaven;
can hardly explain even
why the whitethroat sings on
certain days only.

Each odd discrepancy
issues from afar, and
among the family toys
and gatherings I see
kind Greatie at 93

leaning secretly near
one sunny Easter morning
and whispering, "The rain
is making so much noise.
Doesn't it bother you, dear?"

*

I say a dream is like
an ancient olive tree
that never dies, sending
continuous roots out
underground before I wake,

before the dreamer wakes,
roots popping up forever
to make new olive trees
on other grounds. Asleep
I let a wild red fox

slip from his hedge at dawn,
pause, sniff the gorse and break
into an easy trot
across an open field heedless
of any hunter's plan.

Although his talk was always
superficial, my grandfather
had kindness and good humor.
I liked his lackadaisical
half-penurious ways,

I liked his motorboat
called Puffin, often moored
all morning, all day long
and riding pointlessly
the harbor waves—and yet

once early every summer
my grandfather and brother
and I, beyond Mosquito
and Green and Little Green,
pulled cod from the deep water.

*

Blizzard.... Mount Auburn Street.
Spivack's Antiques Shop open
and the river partially frozen.
Apartments and grocery store
haven't been torn up yet.

From a corner the Old Poet
(as later I'll learn) watches,
watches me talk and dicker.
At length he ambles over.
"You're getting the stuffed parrot?"

"No," I explain, "I'm going
to buy the opium pipe."
The camera pulls away
from the shop and street and city
and childhood. Deeply it's snowing.

II

The young fall in love instantly,
as surely as the stars
rise and a whippoorwill
calls nightly, just before nine.
And as for himself, he

sees her walking the market
square and talking to someone
who doesn't look familiar
before she approaches the theater,
or is she buying a ticket?

An old and bitter-sweet story,
to fall in love instantly.
Later it was the way
she sat at table, her hands.
He was no longer free.

*

Letting her underthings
drop to the floor, she puts on
a bathing suit—it's tight
in the crotch. Okay, let 'em watch
and see how the cloth clings.

Now she pretends to be
oblivious, swinging her legs
over the beach and circling
volleyballers, who are proud of
their tight buns probably.

She is outside and inside
herself simultaneously.
She is playing volleyball.
She is eating a hot dog.
She is swimming with the tide.

First only a few feathers
of darkness,
which you can brush from your eyes.
Then in that fluttering it
gets darker still, as sleek as

onyx, soft as velvet.
Starting in darkness it
gets darker until it grows
enveloping—until
a deep envelope of night

is sealed. Is there a letter
deeper that you haven't read yet?
Maybe. Starting in darkness
it gets darker. Staying
in darkness it gets darker.

*

I feel them both—a warm
breeze and the leftover
coolness of 5 AM
as I begin to jog
down from the sleepy farm.

Temperature comes in layers,
one wafted on another.
Oh it'll be a scorcher,
I can assume already
from the two airs.

Empty and quiet, only
the faintest forest birdsong,
this is the one untrammeled
hour the whole day long.
You wouldn't call it lonely.

I wish I could find an answer
in the articulate grass
to satisfy me finally.
I call the grass articulate
because at dusk I hear

crickets that almost sound
like your heels—the sliding click
of heels as you left and entered
the subway—and I've seen
a mole running underground,

an occasional sparrow pecking
for seed, and also in certain
areas ants. But I don't,
don't see an answer beyond
these ordinary things.

*

Better to wear your sword
as long as you can, George Fox
advises. Another man calls
it better to be a violent
fool than to be a coward.

It's all a process, done
imperfectly at best,
like giving up your ego:
you need an ego first
and preferably a good one.

Nothing you want is false
or stupid, even a sun
shining without clouds. In nature
the bud grows, the flower
breaks, the leaf falls.

Nor are the 59
slogans of Atisha
to be ignored. Some run:
Rest in the nature of alaya,
the essence. In post-meditation

be a child of illusion.
Don't talk about injured limbs.
Abandon hope of fruition.
Meditate on whatever
provokes resentment. Train

without bias in all areas.
Don't misinterpret. Don't
vacillate. Train whole-heartedly.
Don't wallow in self-pity.
Don't expect applause.

*

The piano she has moved
to the far corner of the living room
is the family's walnut upright
that casts away the gloom
of memories she loved.

It's full of the quaint songs
that somehow she doesn't hear
right now—old songs that wait
in readiness, like "Peg o' My Heart,"
torn sheet music that belongs

to herself now. The piano
is versatile, telling her of
grandparents and her childhood,
a farmhouse. Some nights it contains
all she wants to know.

Some have taken the lapse
seriously, of Good and Evil,
that disappearing act,
but him, he hardly minds it,
pondering in his cups

the earlier way it was.
Now laundry flaps on a bough;
days wrinkle and blow—
nothing of any particular
use or value. Does

this bother him much? Not very.
He draws bathwater and
steps in. He washes. Brushes
his teeth. The moon
rises like a berry.

*

Say you're meandering
all day upcountry when
you fall into a maze
of hedges you get lost in
trailing a gold string.

You find a creature sleeping.
Day is almost done,
and as a glazed eye opens
you see only a black sun
and hear a distant clipping

and frantically at nightfall
follow the gold string out.
Try as you will to wake
you join us in the maze,
oh brother animal.

When a kaleidoscope
that was the world's toy breaks
and spills out glass there is
no good looking for pictures
or scooping the glass up,

no good, the pieces don't
even reflect light now
but lie cloudy and dull, as if
swirls of scattering seawater
had left them irrelevant

to anything else here,
lost and cloudy and dull,
and we can remember only
familiar patterns, like
a land immersed in war.

*

The underground is good.
Purgatory and Hell
are here above, flourishing
their dark flowers of evil.
All shall be understood

as we drop underground.
Today I see a girl
dialing a telephone.
She knows from the I.D.
somebody else has phoned

but doesn't recognize
the number. What cannot
be said cannot be said,
and she is alive, not dead.
Heaven is in her eyes.

III

I can hardly see you
with the light off, but I see
our tank illuminated,
hear its buzzing. I see
a blue and orange fish who

flickers a plume of gills,
easing its lacy way
through weeds and compatriots
down to the fallen feed
and yellow pebbles,

down to those pebbles we
sifted the other day,
down through the greenery
and tufts and wafting bubbles
to make a discovery.

*

These are the warm shadows
we like to anticipate
riding over sea
and hill and city
as the brief summer goes.

Our trees begin to blow
at night with less to say.
The ruffled branches make
on every lawn
their usual little dumb-show

no less shadowy than
our bedroom windowshade
caging the moonlight, no
less shadowy than the words
I write, pages I turn.

Rubbing my eyes and nearly
half awake I stumble
down to the living room
and rub my eyes again.
You must have got up early

to bring back violets
and small wildflowers wet
with dew (these early sunrises
in summers seem to be more
enticing than the sunsets).

Your kindness is a given,
but where are you now? I take
my usual coffee, sit
where you have kept our living
room a room to live in.

*

"Oh, no, the intellectual
cannot be happy," so gurus
are claiming time and again
and always I think they mean
me, singling me out. Well,

I have thought long on this,
having taken many a lump
from gurus. Sure, I analyze
and think, and sometimes even
over a nightcap pause

to ponder the Final Cause.
I go to bed serene.
I wake up ready to jump
for joy. Perhaps I'm not
as smart as I thought I was.

Like a mobile over
a crib in Kentucky once
my early tales are lost
to you, of Policeman
Parker, the undercover

savior of little Peebo
who always wandered off
too far and became lost.
Ritual stories. Quietly
told, they gave a placebo

effect to the bedtime air
balancing like the muted
red and blue and magenta
ovals and hearts that moved
you to sleep like prayer.

*

My daughter felt that poison
ivy would float off the leaves
and *kill* by fuming the air
with gas—when she was five
or six—and for this reason

despite my disclaimers, each
of us agreed to give
that area a wide berth,
letting the groundcover sprawl.
Another "sinister patch"

lay near our property
shiny tight-curled in spring
and redder and rich in fall.
Passing in mid-July
we took hands and moved quickly.

Mrs. Christie hopes we'll
forget she dipped into the mind
of the murderer early on,
not very long or much, but
enough to have cheated a little,

fueling a sympathy for
Evil—a sympathy not
quite right, my son will agree,
listening carefully now,
his eyes on a ceiling-crack or

a shaded window. We're
not talking Roger Ackroyd
or the detective-murderer here,
which the bedtime boy and I
consider entirely fair.

*

In praise of folly?—yes,
we knew it once. Better
than spinning a reason out
or needing to be right.
Better than loneliness.

Folly is folly. It brings
a father's photographs,
and wrapped in ribbons are
a mother's diaries
when you said funny things.

One summer standing after
a shower as breezes rippled
tall grass and all
the flowers bent your way
you heard an endless laughter.

The double-chalice of
the sand timer that came
with our new Scrabble set
is fine but irrelevant.
It's simpler to forgive

the waiting turn to turn,
although as I shuffle a few
letters around for want
of anything better to do
in the interim, I imagine

pebble and rock and boulder
and sand of those ancient
generations of aborigines
who also awaited the word,
feeling the years turn over.

*

God of unknown, of days
unlimited—although
how limited they seem!—
I must apologize
for my unsettled ways.

And yet God made me so,
the way I am. And of
the many things I've done
badly, daughter, I must
apologize to you

for any sufferings
created by my words
one angry evening. Trust
is so easily wiped away
like dust on dragonfly wings.

Now the mirror only
belittles the face, and explains
nothing of time or place
or reason for pains.
The favorite statue by

Degas, La Petite Danseuse
—a photo above the jars—
quietly gives the lie
to real ballet slippers here.
Never is there applause;

a compliment brings tears.
Young girl tying her hair.
Oh where is the dance,
where is the dancer's grace,
thought to come with years?

*

Still there is only one
garden for each of us
whose light falls perfectly.
Although this garden slips
away it is not forgotten,

and while we carry many
bundles of flowers from one
new garden to another,
I want to tell you, children,
you won't discover any

to outdo the first
that lay unpicked and waiting.
Remember: there is only
one garden where the moon
came up and the sun burst.

IV

Our neighborhood is changing
for the better in some ways—
fine people, fewer trees
to shed in November. Still
I'd rather be arranging

another trip. I like
ruins and sacred places.
Once there was Avebury
where our kids tumbled around
all afternoon before dark,

barrow, menhir, down,
the stones hewn roughly up
on hills, you couldn't see
them all at once, a motion
furtively serpentine.

*

The Burren is a great
ancient grayness of rock
here in southern Ireland
where you would never expect
something so desolate

and barren to support
a single grass tuft, much less
the 300 varieties
of tiny wildflowers
people have counted, but

one morning when I got
up early to see the sunrise
skimming a part of it
I found wet pockets gathered
at dawn or in the night.

Mairena offers no bar
or café in October, only
small dogs that growl and nip
ankles as you pass by,
wondering who you are.

You're nobody, going up
to a church that isn't ringing
in this scruffy off-the-road
non-touristy village in Spain
where you happened to stop.

But it's unspoiled, the ways
and houses hardly seem
to have changed in decades,
and olive trees still rustle
until the mild wind dies.

*

The long river of Prague
flows under the Charles Bridge.
On a spring dawn I stood
with my camera alone
doing a travelogue

of emerging statuary,
outlines, a finger in the air,
a cross of thorns—they came
as brutal, vigilant figures
faithful against the sky

and waters brightening Prague.
Later my wife and I
moved among tourists and local
children to watch a woman
painting an Easter egg.

In the low-lit chapel
of bones adjoining Evora's
Igreja de Sao Francisco
that a nearly forgotten monk
of 16th century Portugal

set up for meditation
on our dusty life and death,
more than a thousand-odd
skulls pocketed and groined
into the wall (and even

a hanging skeleton)
won't take your breath away,
but they hold the mind
long after you come out
again into the sunshine.

*

It makes me think how long
life is, trudging from room
to room of Toltec, Aztec, Mayan
deities, figures, tombs
and trinkets a million strong!

If I were to drop dead
looking at these things
and they put me under glass
with my tote bag, would gazers
from a later period

look down at me and guess
how dazed I was? how weary?
or note how little our skill
of aesthetics has moved on
to confront or comfort us?

In England where we chose
to rent, bats were at first content
to do their dusky riffs
in summer trees of our back
garden. Now I confuse

them sitting out to gaze.
Less openly they come
as clots that man was made from,
like floaters in ancient eyes,
small-fisted travelers

edgy and errandless.
Bats are the only creatures
below man that know jazz,
that know what jazz is,
can plummet and improvise.

V

It may boil down to your hat,
whether it's wintry or spring-like,
jaunty or all adroop,
whether it's sitting straight
or vaguely angled. Not,

perhaps, for your care and quiet
response and generosity
to children and shy people
will you be remembered, as you
had hoped. Sadly your fate

may boil down to your hat,
whether it's tartan or plain
or deeply feathered, whether
you take it off as soon
as you enter—and that's that.

*

So here's the interior's
window, the dusty bench
and table—hardly more
than a charcoaled fireplace
sealed up for many years,

an old familiar shack.
It's been awhile since anyone
lit a night fire here.
Even spiders are gone
that got in through a crack

leaving an antimacassar
lacework loosely swaying
to our half-open door.
White webs here and there
blow like an old man's hair.

We came to another signpost
and turned to hear brook water
across something like a field—
so hard to reconstruct
the path exactly. At best

we could abandon the macadam
where once the old gentleman walked
who never spoke to us,
but that was long ago,
those summers of our Eden

when, casual or adroit,
after a long day's study
all of us swam together.
I can remember leaping
into the falls at night.

*

The sea being inside
the river itself, where she had caught
a little silver trout?
The day was over; I thought
of many who had died

until I was less myself
than usual—friends and men
and women of fine repute
as guides and a pretty singer
smiling across the gulf.

No, it is never enough
to remember and praise
the old cabin, whiskey and song
past midnight, two o'clock,
a girl wandering off.

Idly she doodles right
triangles, parallel bars
and sectors, blackening
tangent-circles like the eyes
of animals. At night

against her insomnia
she keeps a book of Euclid
by her bed, but never
lights the table lamp.
Instead, an architecture

blossoms in her head:
houses diminishing
down a road, a kitchen
with a gas ring, an eating
nook, and the sky red.

*

Did no Great Spirit come
to me and I accomplish
nothing remarkable
in a good life I wouldn't
call torrid or tiresome?

My life? My life has been
remarkably ordinary
in most respects. In most
respects, rather than out of
step I have been in.

Tonight I saw the hawks
sitting in trees—was on
my way to chaperone
a dance, a local dance,
guarding the younger folks.

She found there was nothing quite
so comfortable as dawn,
a coffee cup and book,
dark islands, a flecked horizon
emerging out of the night

as the sky reddened up
to a half-pleasant draftiness
and again the old windowpanes
of squiggles and thin mullions
that would leak rain. Her cup

she'd lift to the true gods of dawn
and to lobster boats leaving.
Often it troubled her
to imagine what would come
of this place when she was gone.

*

Beacon Hill: good food
and elevator, mirrors, spiral
banister and high-spoked
circular skylight gazing
down at me since babyhood.

But what I cared for most
was not those Sunday lunches
or even the gong mannequin
my younger brother loved,
but later, as we crossed

the Charles, the evening skyline
and a first glimpse of home's
gateway to Cambridge: it
was like a little toy
lit up and truly mine.

You can't go home again?
But who would say so when
everything comes round
as it did, as it will again,
and you are young and clean

and to "Mood Indigo"
or maybe a late Beethoven
quartet you look up from
your paper and, out the window,
you see the initial snow

fall, as it did, again,
barely accumulating,
and any door can open
and a small son and daughter
run in, run in?

*

My graying head I find
complex, though people say
I just don't look my age.
Hard to believe. Fingers
less flexible, the mind

forgetful, the poor feet
soft and sore if I press
the appropriate indents
suggesting "liver impact,"
"kidney issues." The prostate,

frankly, has given me more
runaround than everything else
combined. The later body
gets quarrelsome. It's just
that it hung so loose before.

My father under the Gainsborough
and to one side of the Wyeth
reviews our inheritance
and mixes anecdotes
with his loneliness and sorrow.

We drive to visit him once
a week, my wife and I
(my brother living closer).
Like most of us he mingles
dream and reminiscence.

It's like his grandfather's "The Story
of a Bad Boy," mostly untrue,
trumping up incidents
like the oarless little schoolboy
floating out to sea.

*

When there is very little
time left, the clock appears
to slow down. A leaf forever
from the tree-top weaves its
slow-motion ritual

downward bough by bough
swaying through air that comes
heavier day by day now
beyond his windowsill,
and ah the hour is slow

as cones lie scattered on
soft needles, and the fir trees
gaze from their shallow roots.
Upmeadow a young boy
kicks windfalls where they've fallen.

Where the Unconscious seems
to greet us equally,
morning and evening meet.
We are the Contraries.
We are the one who dreams.

Two Japanese ladies
newly awake (it seems)
have floated down from the garden
down from the bat garden
after a shower to close

their parasols
and lift up fluted silk
kimonos now and later
undo their delicate feet
and step into pools.

*

The first people stay alive
as they were, although gone
and no longer beautiful
and young and talking, laughing,
in tears. Yet they survive

indelible, holy, the soul
of everything I remember,
the worst and best of scattered
moments. Just the other
day it struck me the whole

puzzle works in reverse.
No wonder I feel disjointed
when I stop to contemplate
fragments of me throughout
the world—the universe.

What we have thrown away,
and what our children, too,
will throw away—those things
that enter the endless dark—
is a mystery today.

Perhaps the mystery
itself is what we threw
away—the whippoorwills
and morning glories and trees
and fireflies? Certainly

I threw away a boy
running in country dust
to the mailbox for *PM*
and its cartoon "Barnaby"
that brought a simple joy.

                    *

At night return the place-names:
Brattle Street and Rose,
Berea and Cape Elizabeth,
Tivoli, Oslo, Highgate,
Hampstead, the river Thames,

and while they often glimmer
at night or anywhere
to buffer and affirm
our little lives' appearance,
finally they don't cover

much time or area
but simply hang in air,
names as clear and fragrant
and cryptic as the Hanging
Gardens of Babylonia.

A rain begins to fall
on chairs of a summer lawn
on warm summer afternoons,
and now on summer nights
I hear its casual

patter soaking the ground,
the turn-around and road
and fields somewhere beyond
the precincts where I hold
you close. I like the sound.

We have only begun to know
our lives slipping away
like rain on summer chairs
on summer nights that began
to happen long ago.

from
THE DEATH OF MICHELANGELO

INTRODUCTION

Michelangelo was a great sculptor and architect, an excellent painter, a good poet, and an often grouchy man. He had few friends, although he much admired one of them, the widowed Vittoria Colonna, and probably sexually loved a number of men. He disliked the insular five years of painting the Sistine Chapel for the tyrannical Pope Julius II. Even more painful to him was his inability ever to satisfy his father, a successful businessman who neither understood nor approved his son's profession, even when the money began to flow in.

He hated and fought the aging process, although it helped to bring about his important conversion from Neoplatonism (the idea that earthly beauty rises above) to his late Christianity. In the last of these loosely translated sonnets (some include information from his letters) we see him creating his perhaps finest sculpture, the Rondanini pietà, whose strange incompleteness, beautiful in itself, is the result of his catching cold in the rain and dying, at 89, from his nightly horse ride.

TO VITTORIA COLONNA

The beauty that I wanted, was it in
myself only, so that I lost my days
to some mistaken dream, seeing your face
in sculpture as the stone broke open?
Or was it actual and truly yours,
binding me to you in our mortal pain,
then spreading everywhere, now here, now gone,
that took my helpless days and took my peace,

God having made me all one open eye?
Beauty, perhaps, is really paradise's
far from our living, holier and chaste,
yet risen from us, and the reason I
ran back burning under your eyelashes
looking always where I loved you first.

IN THE SISTINE CHAPEL

It gave me such a goiter dangling there
as cats get drinking streams in Lombardy,
stray wanderers, I felt my swollen belly
under my chin, more troubles than I'd care
to repeat or remember, huddled, beard to the sky,
the scaffold fixed to fool that wretch Bramante
(who wanted all the holes to show), my hair
dribbling a sticky fresco, paint in the eye

and down my harpy's chest, skin taut up front
and folded into bags behind, my rear
slung numbly outward as a counterweighter,
I must have looked like a blind peashooter, bent
like a Syrian bow, with one thing clear:
that chapel a sad place, and I no painter.

FOR DANTE

Or think of Dante. Out of cloud and sky
the poet came and saw with mortal eyes
our twin hells of the just and good, and rose
alive, to God again, where he should be.
For this bright star I can suppose it was
a time no worse or better than our day,
we share a kindred destiny, though he
rose through all evils till he saw the stars.

The glorious poem he left us goes unknown
today back in our nest, ungrateful Florence,
who crucify the blessed of this world.
Yet to be Dante! For an hour to own
his eyes, to borrow even half his glance,
I would give this world up and be exiled.

ON CREATION

He who created, before time began—
before the earth with its unfolding marble—
time itself, later split time double,
lending the higher portion to the sun,
the low and nearer to the moon, so all
in a single stroke gave luck or fortune
to everyone, to me only the brown
soft time familiar at my birth and cradle.

If I am anything at all, it comes
of being born in that high mountain air
echoing far to the stonecutter's blow
I took in with my nurse's milk; it comes
of open summer days in the Carrara
quarries, marble floating up the Arno.

TO TOMMASO

You knew, my lord, that I knew that you knew
I had come back again to see beauty.
You knew that we both knew, to put it plainly,
the one of us who mirrors God is you.
Two spirits who have loved in spirit surely
should keep wide-open doors, or if not, why
not tell me why? You knew, my lord, a way
to keep an old man doubly sorry.

My own door sign, "Whoever comes in May
can ask no more than leaves"—perhaps it catches
a little of my late unhappiness?
Think of me as a moon in the night sky
shining only where the far sun brushes.
I knew, Tommaso, how it was your eyes.

TO HIS FATHER

Too many years now I am left behind
feeling whatever makes grief stay and stay
at your death following my brother's. He,
your son, my brother, is painted on my mind
but *you* are sculpted in my heart. Ninety
summers were given you here to understand,
Father, growing frailer and wise and kind
before your last sun sank into the sea.

All my lifetime work was done for you.
Now more and more, it seems, I ask
to greet you steady in unchanging light,
to learn my death from yours, as I pursue
my simple livelihood down here where dusk
always darkens, and morning turns to heat.

ON AGING

Giants leave stinking meats at my doorsill.
Be off with them! I have become Arachne's
homework in this little gravesite, gravehouse
where I wait in fear. A fuzzy wind rattles
out one hole or another. If I wheeze
too much, a morning's urine chortles
down old pipes; if my soul could smell my spittle
now it would not allow this bread and cheese.

I terrify people, I am lumbago bones
with teeth like an old keyboard's falling out.
A spider and a cricket have taken up
residence in my ears, one spins
cocoons, the other chirps all night.
I cannot sleep.

ON HIS CONVERSION

Across a wind-swept sea and open current
my fragile boat is arrived already
to a common port, by this long journey
full of sin, to make a last account.
Gone now, I say, my affectionate fantasy
of Art as earthly king, that sweet tyrant
men may want, against our wills may want,
yet in the end see God so far away.

And my once happy vanity, how will it
help me now while my slow double-ending comes,
if soul and body both go as life goes?
My art was mere puppetry. It cannot quiet
a soul turning to that Love whose arms
opened once, to take us, on the cross.

THE RONDANINI

The dome. It gathers air,
but here in my studio I would join
my God quietly. I work for pardon.
All day there are too many noises.
Pitiful only to *begin* to learn my work
so late when I am dying. Nothing is done—
a candle on my cap at night flickers on this
shadowy thin pietà. I knocked some pieces

to the floor. Little is right,
here and outside, everywhere—stupidities
and loss surround me. Now better not
to speak, to be quiet, to sleep, to be
numb while layers slide off, days go, voices
fall away. Make me the stone.

from
SONNETS FOR GRIMM

BLUE SHOES

Cinderella, Cinderella, that
was a long way to go to get nothing!
Home again, you are the sweetest thing.
Home again, what are you looking at
but a glass slipper in your sooty hand,
a slipper you can think of as a cool
reminder, as a blue leftover jewel,
a single slipper in your little hand?

A single slipper in . . . oh, if it wraps
your own heel's milkiness and toes' pallor
on this calm aftermorning of collapse
like washed-up bottle seaglass, Cinderella,
consider the translucent blue. Perhaps
it was the impurities that gave it color.

A RIDDLE

Three ladies had been changed into flowers
blooming together in a meadow, but
one flower was allowed in later hours
(the others sleeping) to go home at night.
Once on a dewy hour of daybreak
when from her husband she must steal away
she said, *If you will only come and pick
me early in the meadow, I can stay
with you always*. But since they looked alike
and equally in bloom when he arrived there
(their petals very colorful but alike!)
how could he know his own among the other
flowers, although he did without mistake?

Because the dew had not fallen on her.

THE WICKED HEALER

"Cure ill—by ill," the crone said,
with a benevolent poke.
"If the night makes you afraid
go out into the dark
Seek out the darkest hole
in the forest you can find
and when you find that hole
stick in your hand."

"And . . . for claustrophobia?"
"Find a bat-hung cavern
or cave and huddle there
until you are saved, my good man!"
"And if I can't get air?"
"Expel what air you can."

EVEN THE WIZARD WONDERING

Over his sill a pale dawn comes to fill
a chamber saved for light, maybe to overflow.
He has not slept. He has nowhere to go.
As for lying abed, he may as well.
The early songbirds twitter. But it's all
a balancing act, as cap and bells tinkle
far in some drafty hollow of the castle
where sconces flutter, where another scroll-
like day spills out along the Royal Hall
and turrets he imagines beyond view
to cultivate a calm as roses do.
It's all a balancing act. For while his skill
at divination and his power to sway
increase withal, he has so little to say.

THE CRUEL MOTHER

"Mother, in no stories nowadays do
I find a lithe staircase
spiraling down from a cupola skylight
like a shard of glass;
nor can I legend a leaf
on the lawns of our palace
to swirl anymore down to
the green grass."

"Son, no more will your life
turn on a wish or belief—
or not the lot of it.
The bird of Joy will not come
to your life. The bottom
has fallen out of it."

HOMEWARD

No bother is it for a knight at arms
to sing, dropping his happy coins
of thought and love along the horsetrotted
roadway, letting his hawk untethered fly
ahead to scout the grass, with talons
curled and pointed, now that a hundred wars
are done! his futile wars all over
and a new age for lack of battlefronts
carries him homeward by the fields unpursed
and colored in medieval buttercups
of dotted yellow and such green seasons
lying out before him stubbornly young.
A split, a gap, a rupture, an abyss
waits for the unwary nonetheless.

BROTHER IN THE WELL

How can you climb out of a well if thrown
by your drunken stepbrothers into it?
Cool and damp and soft is the moss underfoot,
and every twig crinkles crisp as a bone.
Already it is evening. Off to a tavern
and whipping their steeds on to a frenzy no doubt,
eager to pass the pitcher and give a shout,
go the stepbrothers who assumed you would drown.

The circular wall is sheer that surrounds you.
Crickets begin—oblivious. At no loss
in their circuit drift little stars above you.
Until this moment where was loneliness?
Where was the danger of seclusion? You
are like sediment at the bottom of a glass.

THE MIRROR

It haunts him. He lies in the dark
fearing to see it. He fears the gold
frame that carries no nick
although he has bumped it sevenfold.
He fears the glass, warm
to a turned knuckle or the back of his hand
as he tests it in the sitting room.
He knows he is deemed dull and
unworthy by this mirror.
Twice he was gazing into it
and found that he didn't appear
in the glass, which only caught
the sitting room behind him where
in the sunlight somebody sat.

ASHPUTTLE

I read to my daughter in the Manheim version:
When winter came, the snow spread
a white cloth over the grave, and when
spring took it off, the man remarried.
No, this tale is not about your father, dear.
"Father," she said, "break off the first
branch that brushes against your hat
on your way home, and bring it to me."
But now I see you are growing sleepier.
After thanking him, she went to her
mother's grave and planted the hazel
sprig over it and cried so hard that
tears fell and watered it, and so it
grew and became a beautiful tree.

THE SWANS

What is our way into the dream? a twill
of words unweaving, an image of a girl
who could be anyone under a spell?

A princess was commanded for six years
never to speak, but to sew starflowers
into shirts for her six brothers

who had been transformed into dreamy swans
by a wicked witch, and all the pains
of the princess would be wasted if she spoke once.

Hearing this, she quit her hut in the forest
and climbed a tree and hid the rest
of the night there, for the world is very unjust.

Next morning she climbed down and (as you know)
gathered starflowers and began to sew.

FLACKER IN PARIS

For a time the young Samuel Beckett acted as secretary to his idol, James Joyce. This poem is much fictionalized (for example, the two men are philosophers), but suggested by real events in that relationship.
    —J.A.

Flacker forsook the Emerald Isle
and took his swelling work-in-progress—
"Notations Toward a Proof of God"—
to Paris where the ex-pat Danish
philosopher Ramsay Dalton lived.
By any measure Flacker's book was odd.

Odd, too, in aspects physical
was he: tall and emaciated,
pale and craggy, as opposed
to Dalton's roly-poly, sit-back
air of jovial complaisance.
In Dalton's mind philosophy was closed.

But Flacker wanted commendation,
argument, on certain issues—
with Dalton, famous hedonist
and atheist and party-giver
and local toast of Paris, being
first and foremost on shy Flacker's list.

It was a pleasant day, like waves
of water flowing over you.
Behind him lay the rainy nation
that made him put his thoughts in order.
He'd written Dalton earlier,
received a coolish, open invitation.

So after renting modest digs
in some unfashionable arrondissement
and setting a specific date,
he took his work across the Seine
and walked down Dalton's shady nook
that afternoon in spring of '88

only to be jumped by one
who hunkered in the bushes hoping

that here was something valuable—
money perhaps?—and pummeled Flacker
and, grabbing the fat briefcase, ran,
not leaving Flacker any chance to call.

No bones were broken, but the blood
spattered his shirtfront as he rose
and limped along and nearly passed
the public garden into which
apparently the thief had tossed
his briefcase and its contents in disgust.

Some of his papers blew among
the ferns and tulips, some were lost
forever, though he gathered up
what did remain. He wouldn't have
pressed charges anyhow, knowing
some sorrow is impossible to stop.

But what a mess! Two ingenues
detained him at the hotel desk,
startled enough to halt their patter,
seeing dark resultant clots
of blood that stained his rumpled outfit,
not wanting him to ride the elevator.

Finally they agreed to summon
the concierge by intercom,
and from an aperture there came
a dapper little Frenchman sporting
an eyepatch on one eye, who now
in courtly tones asked Flacker for his name.

Whether by his insistence or
his obvious sincerity
Flacker rode to the top floor
alone, disreputable-appearing,

and with his briefcase now intact
walked down the hall and buzzed the oaken door.

> Perhaps the year's tone was set by our first meeting. Flacker had not dressed for the occasion. He seemed both disheveled and mentally distracted. As for me, having received missives from him, admiring ones from Ireland and specific requests from Paris (he had settled on the Left Bank) I did my best to set him at ease—as did my wife, Patricia, serving excellent sandwiches and tea. But the young fellow seemed determined to leave, to cover his *gaucheries*, from the minute he entered the apartment, dropping silverware, napkins, and finally his own battered briefcase spilling papers on our floor. Barely could I enjoy his odd lack of aplomb, myself willing at the same time to delay any judgment on this person who seemed to be taking advantage of our hospitality.
> —from Ramsay Dalton's essay, "My Time with George Flacker"

One can imagine Dalton—surely
one does, one does imagine Dalton;
also his wife and thirty-two-
year-old unmarried daughter, quite
a household pictured in the glossies
living above the Seine to a perfect view.

Of what use was a perfect view
to Dalton, who was losing eyesight?
Consider Dalton's coterie:
First Fridays of the Month, a philosophers'
gathering here for cheer and song
and lights along the Seine above the city.

"Ah, Mr. Flacker, sad to see
you looking—oh, the worse for wear.
But why not enter." Dalton's greeting!
"You must be wanting to get home
and change. But stay for a quick tea?"
Hardly as Flacker had visualized their meeting.

In such a posh apartment, Flacker
found it hard to talk, and hard
to know what Dalton's laughter meant.
They spoke of God, the universe,
as Dalton, crossing ankles, smiled:
"An ominous silence shrouded the event."

When Flacker rose to go, his briefcase
opened inadvertently,
spewing out his papers once
again. "Tut tut!" said Dalton, musing,
somehow consenting, though, to keep
them for perusal if he got the chance.

> Now came, perhaps, my second mistake, though I cannot blame myself for it. With my well-known failing eyesight, I required a helper to put my work in order. Cecilia, my daughter, had dropped away as a possibility after some clearly futile sessions, whereas Flacker had dealt with philosophical matters throughout his brief life. Further, as I learned on our next meeting (I was generous enough to invite him back), he could translate rather skillfully into French, as none of us ex-patriots could manage at the time, and claimed a readiness to work without pay, "just to be near you," as he admitted. I have a sentimental streak, despite the tight logic and formality in my philosophical system.
> —Ibid.

Dalton's philosophy was so
obscure that people flocked to buy
his books and, in the old days, fill
the lecture halls. Generally
only the first sentence—often
a question anyhow—was understandable.

But here was something Dalton wanted.
He wanted a new secretary,
his publisher eager for a great
"Dalton Reader—Layman Style,"

with freshly-written "chapter links"
for which young Flacker stepped up to the plate.

Typically before they got
work-sessions underway, Dalton's
melancholic daughter, Cecilia,
leaned by a window or the door jam,
maybe thrusting a hip out, staring
at them or nothing in particular.

Dalton indulged his dark-haired daughter
(so Flacker figured) by delay
in asking her to leave the study.
This made for daily consternation.
It seemed she had a history
of deep depression (but didn't everybody?).

Why let her in at all? And why
such later lack of clarity
and bouts of anger? One didn't ask.
The work-lights blazing for his eyes,
a vaporizer for his asthma:
being his secretary was no easy task.

This moody watcher made it worse,
smiling and drifting. Flacker felt
she pinned on *him* a wistful gaze,
Dalton oblivious. "I won't
have people speaking ill of her.
In certain ways Cecilia is my muse."

When she wearied, one eye drifted.
Flacker didn't relish her wistful
gazes, though he must admit,
on a lonely aperitif at night
and a small entree as he reviewed
the day's experience, he, too, felt split.

He imagined feathery presences
that were perhaps just feathery parts
of himself issuing from
his head and heart and genitals
to flutter about him, bringing him
to the verge of insanity and inner doom. . . .

Cities are different, or the same
if you are the same in them.
After his supper all alone
he sat below the Arc de Triomphe
for cheese-plate or a slow espresso
or walked in singleness along the Seine.

I am too absent for this world
he thought, *too delicate and frail.*
I long for everything that's gone,
but never liked it at the time,
never enjoyed the songs and books
and people and places that I've come to mourn.

Why was he here? Why *was* he here?
Here for his mother who had shut
him from her heart so long ago?
He didn't like to think this way.
Or think of *her*. How life can make
us writhe to hide what coverings we do!

He valued privacy, he liked
Nature, the emptier the better,
somewhere perhaps the perfect void;
he liked to imagine rain falling
on hills where sheep had grazed, with dew
and mist and oceans rolling under God.

Tabula rasa of the soul.
The bits and pieces pressuring him

were only windfall night-and-day
remnants of this earthly world.
"Now that our fate has been foretold,
Sweet Seine, flow gently till I end my stay."

> . . . nor could I keep him from turning certain sessions into a sort of amusement.
> He seemed, from time to time, unwilling or unable to commit on essential
> matters. . . .
> —Ibid.

Flacker—who worked so seriously.
Mornings when he arrived at nine
he hardly knew what to assume.
One day he found the music up,
shades down, and Dalton with his cane
doing a little jig around the room.

During that session Dalton rambled,
"How I love women! Cecilia—yes,
she was my secretary *once*.
It didn't work. . . . Keep women near me!
We're animals, Flacker, that's a fact,
sometimes we only think of pricks and cunts."

Another day: "My dear papa
was too material. They say
'material' equates with 'mothers'.
The old boy put a premium
on *money*. Used it in a way
to paralyze himself and control others."

Flacker hoped to swing the banter
back to something deeper—Life,
the long arm of particulars,
Creation and Astronomy
together, so by metaphor
implying God as sun among the stars.

"We love the sunlight, not the sun!
Not even sunlight, Flacker, but
the trickle-down effect of it."
Whenever Flacker spoke about
Origins, God, Reality,
Dalton would parry with acerbic wit.

Or else if Flacker gingerly
approached the subject of *his* book
(knowing no answer was deserved),
other than ceding that he "liked
the premise well enough," the great
philosopher turned silent and reserved.

If simple truth be told, Dalton
had never cracked that manuscript
of Flacker's, so one summer night,
specs on, with extra table light,
he did so ... ! *Brilliant* ... ! *Brilliant* ... !! how
it cast a new simplicity and insight—

resolved old issues! brought
a new and fresh—he closed the book
and put the thing away again.
He promptly shut the roll-top desk;
a certain anger welled up in him.
For hours he sat there in the same position.

Yet a real fondness had sprung up
between them: Dalton almost
craved his secretary. Flacker, in turn,
believed that simply being in
the room gave life a Meaning, even
when Dalton talked of eyes and nose and heartburn.

> Oh, it's been written that Flacker became part of the family. Nothing could be further from the truth! I must confess he skillfully wedged himself—through a kind of wheedling that one can detect only in retrospect—into certain social occasions that were initially family affairs. I felt uncomfortable excluding him *ante facto*, and thus I allowed him to tag along....
> —Ibid.

Dalton and his family enjoyed
themselves at social openings,
and though he didn't wish to do it
Flacker often accompanied them,
one opera dragging on and on—
more agony than he could bear ran through it.

But Dalton needed longer breaks
than stage and opera from the irksome
work of putting his Anthology
together. And the cream of these
was his much-touted Friday eves
on which he threw a special raucous party.

These monthly gatherings could take
your mind off anything, laughing
and dancing up a storm. By choice
you drank liqueurs or imported stout,
Cecilia played a Steinway upright
while Dalton sang in his sweet tenor voice.

Great boozy hours of song and cheer.
As usual by midnight most
were shuffling for their coats, and weaving.
But one (whom Dalton thought his own
cohort) discussed *Infinity*
on the couch with Flacker before leaving.

And as the months rolled on—as all
these parties of the month rolled on—
the weaving up and down the hall
began to lessen. With Flacker on
the couch and drawing others to him,
the mood began to turn more philosophical.

> . . . thus, if anything, [Flacker] undermined the "First Fridays." I am not certain why he felt he should attend these parties, or why I permitted it, beyond my own general acceptance of others' wishes. Our friend, simultaneously shy and aggressive (like many of the Irish), would sit on the couch or retire to the kitchen, his gangly presence felt and noted. As I gradually perceived the bloom leaving these gatherings, I called a moratorium until my great Anthology should be completed and Flacker gone forever. . . .
> —Ibid.

Truth is, as Flacker knew, not all
philosophies can deal with God
or ethics, happiness and pain;
yet to refute prevailing views
we must be cognizant of any
thought of thinkers that preceded and remains.

Plato looms large, and Aristotle,
Augustine, Aquinas, the Enlightenment,
Descartes, Spinoza, Schopenhauer,
Hegel certainly, Hume and Kant,
Nietzsche, etc. . . . on and on
right up to Dalton, pundit of the hour.

> Yes, sometimes any record needs to be set straight.
> —Ibid.

For all his personal exchange
with Dalton (which he wouldn't lose
for anything!), where was the core
of Dalton's discourse reasoned out

in the earlier, unpublished work
that Flacker was forbidden to go near?

> Do I alter history? Far from it. Some critics have asserted, in regard to this man, that I wanted a son. Curses on those who think so! (As if one daughter were insufficient.) True enough, Flacker emulated me as a fledgling child might admire a father. But the problem lay, rather, in the fact that, unbeknownst to me, Flacker was making a gruesome but understandable play for Cecilia, who tried her best to fend him off. If I go so far as to fault myself for not spotting the dilemma at once, where, then, were the clues?
> —Ibid.

One day when Flacker knew the rooms
were empty, he came early. Still
he felt the drift of nightly vapors.
He opened drawers and drew the early
essays out. But in the doorway
Cecilia stood! and watched him riffling through the papers.

That girl!—who'd tried ballet and sculpture,
local theatricals, anything to
outshine her mother, Dalton's wife,
but failed at everything (except
piano, at which she wasn't great)
beginning her pursuits too late in life.

"Ah, so . . ." she murmured, gliding near
and lingering there. "My breasts are thought
quite wonderful by those who've seen them."
She lifted up her shift: indeed
her breasts hung full and carroted
as suddenly she pulled his head between them!

"I used to be his secretary . . ."
she murmured, cradling his slack head
from one hard nipple to another.

"I wouldn't want to undermine
relationships, I wouldn't want
to mention any of all this to Father...."

So, under blackmail, there began
their futile and lugubrious
affair—for her, misguided lust
and useless energy—for him
passivity and guilt; almost
a competition who would go mad first.

Those dark, clandestine days went on
and on, as gradually she grew
deep-circled, spectral, jumpy, thin.
Dalton, calling it growing pains,
became outraged and frantic when
his wife, Patricia, brought the doctors in.

> It's clear, in retrospect, that Flacker's behavior pressured my daughter day by day, and eventually she buckled. But even if, as certain critics, in facile hindsight, have suggested, I had removed Flacker earlier, I might only have delayed an endemic problem. Finally, it was my wisdom to send Cecilia back to the old clinic for needed rest and oblivion.
> —Ibid.

Abjectly Flacker felt to blame,
but couldn't speak. And Mrs. Dalton,
lacking facts, could only say
how to our grief Cecelia showed
the awful tell-tale signs of yet
another breakdown if not sent away.

"Can you believe it, Flacker! Can you
conceive it!" Dalton pounded, "a wife
so meanly jealous and self-willed,
so jealous of her daughter's youth

and perspicacity she'd sooner
have her locked up than fulfilled?"

> If any proof of Flacker's blame need be confirmed at this later date, his response to Cecilia's absence spoke volumes. He looked devastated.
> —Ibid.

Infinity! oh shameful sadness!
oh guilt and horror everywhere!
Flacker could hardly lift a pen
to write his name, much less accept
dictation from on high—not that
he ever wished to see that dreadful girl again.

Dalton, too, fell into clumps
of despondency himself. No further
parties turned his spirits bright.
Nor could he think of much to say,
nor manage any "chapter links"
which quiet Flacker tried his best to write.

Yet very oddly, day by day,
the Dalton Reader flourished. Dalton
grew easier and took time off
to have a tad of wine for lunch
(Flacker too weary to indulge),
and smoke occasional cigars and cough.

Nostalgically as Flacker gazed
ahead, he wondered: Now that this
long partnership was almost through,
in retrospect would Dalton ever
look kindly backward, ever say
"Flacker in Paris! . . . I remember you . . ."?

I cannot claim the man was totally insensitive or stupid—such an assertion would be unfair—or that he was entirely unhelpful in completing my "Reader." On the other hand, his so-called philosophy remains inchoate—inherently so, I fear, despite all the attention lavished on his work in recent years. And, despite myself, I had moments when I, too, under his odd presence, actually considered gods other than rigorous form and logic. As soon as my Cecilia came home, however, I returned Flacker's manuscript to him, without remarking on its more than possible flaws.
—Ibid.

A bitter gulf, unbridgeable:
one thinker drawn to the Complex,
the younger to Simplicity
(but only as a final step
of knowledge, giving you release
to throw away the ladder and be free).

And then one afternoon at break time
old Dalton saw that something comes
to all—perhaps a single minute,
perhaps even a fleeting day
or two—when we accept
exactly who we are and we act on it.

For Dalton realized how his young
disciple wove a tapestry
of thought that might catch on—
tying so many strands together!
He smiled at Flacker. Noted! Feeling
happily impotent, Flacker lay down.

Who knows what our coming age will bring. Does anyone? Someone must dream our future into being, and perhaps Flacker himself will be part of it. However, I leave to that noble future my own considerable pages, knowing I

have accomplished much, perhaps indeed my best work, in the past twelve months with him here. I review these months with obvious pride. As for Flacker, we had an almost affectionate parting of the ways. I cannot explain it.
—Ibid.

And briefly, briefly, a contentment
seemed to fill the small apartment
as Dalton pondered, "No surprise
I'm getting on...." For he was ailing:
no longer was it simply failing
eyes. His failing eyes.... His failing eyes.

At last the languid afternoon
gave way and he could barely see
Flacker asleep on the divan.
Mingling his jealousy and love
Dalton forgave himself. "That man
will be remembered after he is gone."

And leaning backward, thought again
in the warm Paris afternoon . . .
"We'll be remembered after we are gone."

from FOAM (A SEQUENCE)

August childhood on the coast of Maine with my grandparents—and later

> *While earth is home*
> *we are its froth*
> *and foam.*

STUDY

Wide, wide, wide is the sea
below my great-grandfather's study.
They say he sat in his study and tried
to write, but gazed at the sea instead.
Never, he said, could he write with such
sea and rocks and trees and birds to watch.

GAMA AND GAMPA

"And the Spirit of God moved upon
the face of the waters," she read to me.
And when she left, I would position
myself to watch, beyond the sea break,
the green light blinking on Whitehead—
as if it were my own to fall asleep by.
Maybe two miles out. "Or three,"
Gampa, often at odds, insisted.

THE TALE OF THE DINGHY

1

A fiberglass dinghy washed up on our rocks
one evening on a bright three-quarter moon
and turning tide. It surprised me and Gama

and Gampa and Mum and Dad and David
and guest Aunt Elsie (Gama's college roommate).

"In point of fact," said Dad, "it surprised everyone."

2

David was half-asleep in his crow's nest,
I was taking a bath downstairs with Gampa
whistling, as often, at the sink and mirror

(his presence always made me feel uneasy
while taking a bath) when sensitive Aunt Elsie

cried out that something had washed up on our rocks.

3

Aunt Elsie couldn't (or wouldn't) pronounce her "r"s,
a mild annoyance to Gama, who believed
she did it for theatrical effect.

It's true Aunt Elsie favored funny phrases.
Instead of saying "I'm going for a short walk"

she'd say, "Farewell, I'm off on a bwief stwoll."

4

And so that night she actually had said,
"Something tewwible has been cawwied
onto our wocks!"—nothing wrong with "wocks,"

of course, for the word seemed inevitable—
and some of us got bundled and hurried down

to check it out (with even David coming).

5

A five-foot dinghy, it could easily take
two passengers, or three if balanced well.
Only one oar, a painter, and no name.

We carried it above the high tide mark,
and then, next morning, to our small side lawn

by the woods, and we inquired around town.

6

No one had filed a missing boat report
and no ordinary boat lacked its dinghy,
(lobstermen often leave them on the mooring),

the fancier yachts even having two or more.
Mum did some notices that we hung up.

I enjoyed seeing the harbor boats at dusk—

7

my favorite, "Second Wind," so like a kayak
narrowed to look both ways, a polished hull
of mahogany and shiny brasswork, an aftermast,

a spinnaker gray with yellow stars on it,
halyards impeccably coiled. It seldom left

the harbor, though, as if our guardian spirit.

8

Dad, a top-notch sailor, disdained the coast guard.
Nearly home one day, our sloop was becalmed,
our motor failing outside their Whitehead station.

We waved and shouted. When finally they came out
they didn't know our harbor! still they hooked

us up, took off, and nearly plowed us under.

9

And so, that later morning after the night
the skiff washed up, we thought (because of Dad's
well-voiced opinion) there'd be no follow-up.

Doubters included me and Mum and Dad
and David and Gama and Gampa—not Aunt Elsie,

who "wefused" to judge the sea's "pwofessionals."

10

But to our admiration, we learned the coast guard
scoured the waters of Penobscot Bay
hoping to find, perhaps, somebody floating

or maybe a craft with its dinghy missing,
and they questioned boats at sea, and traveled on

and finally spotted just one bobbing oar.

11

Though not remarkable (this errant skiff),
the city newspaper sent someone round
to photograph it sitting in our woods

and even published a brief interview—
to little stir. But our painter friend Bob Logan

decided he would do some charcoals of it.

12

Bob, as I recall him, red-haired, tense,
was one who enjoyed series. He must have done
a dozen studies from varying angles,

also an etching plate I own as legacy.
No threat to Andrew Wyeth (whose fame came later)

he painted seriously and loved to laugh.

13

He also liked my Machiavellian humor.
For Gama's birthday I composed an elegy,
"The Wreck of the Dory," with as many "r"s

as I could muster and asked Aunt Elsie to read it
aloud as "cwown of the celebwation."

Bob stifled himself so hard he left to save his bladder.

14

Bob and Gampa were best of buddies, too,
and Ros, his wife, and Gama enjoyed themselves
(though sometimes secretly critiqued each other).

I learned my contract bridge on special late-nights
watching them play at the green felt table

by firelight and cigar puffs going up.

15

By Gampa's indolence the dinghy sat there
day after day, week after week, until
he liked to call it a "sentimental fixture."

At last no one could move it for the dead patch.
David and I half-filled it up with dirt

and grew a Victory Garden of lettuce and carrots.

16

Sooner or later it turned legendary
(the boat I mean—certainly not the garden),
though Gama wanted the whole thing carted off—

it took up cranberry space: okay with me!
just fewer cranberries for us to pick

and spread in the sun for Mary's tangy sauce.

17

Our ancient clunker of a dinghy went in
early to swell the boards and minimize
the slosh we'd tolerate the first few picnics.

I wonder if Dad looks down now on the float
that Mum had wanted but he deemed too pricey.

We'd haul our dinghy out on slimy ropes.

18

But fun—I was allowed to row alone
into the harbor to catch what flounder I could,
which Gama and I would eat the following breakfast.

(I'd collected periwinkles at low tide
and rowed out before noon to drop my line,

and wonderful to feel that little tug.)

19

Dad finally bought a new bright fiberglass
to row us piecemeal out to the Friendship sloop.
He warned Gama to step right in the center.

"Darling, I've been around boats longer than you've
been alive," she said proudly, stepping near the rim,

overturning the boat, and went straight down.

20

Near the end of August the papers reported
that a lobsterman some miles up the coast
had boarded a sailboat anchored over-long

and found old liquor bottles, rotted food,
a Bible, an out-of-date bow-sticker.

Mum was the first to put it all together.

21

I wasn't sad exactly, as today I would be
at any suicide (as we assumed).
I wasn't sad, but I was full of thought.

It was the first time I began to realize
(vaguely) a soul can go, a soul can go

and leave us only with a kind of shell.

HARTS NECK ROAD

Narrow way, mostly dirt.
Gama and old Mrs. Foote,
who both drove snail-like
in the dead center of the road, one morning
at the mailbox turn collided—
a minor jolt.
Happily, on brief inspection, they decided
it was no one's fault.

RICH

Toggle-bottles once
broke into sea glass,
cloudy soft shards to
pick up as I'd pass

below the tide-scribble
of weed, by rock
and pool, to rub like coins
in my pocket.

THE SWAY OF THE SEA

I think the sway of the sea—
I must have been about
eight—got into me
that day on his motorboat
when Gampa let me out

on the giant bell buoy
off Southern Island—the pound
of clappers, the slippery algae
as he circled around,
the boat's wake swelling the up/down.

On foggy days, air soft
and the faraway buoy clanging,
I see myself still clinging
unready to get off.

FAMILY CRUISE

David hard at the tiller, Dad
pointing correct directions out,

Mum in the cabin heating soup,
me on the bowsprit watching the chop—

whatever happens out at sea
these are the halcyon days of gladness.

HYMN-SING

Community Hymn-sing carried on without us
on Sunday summer evenings. Nebulous

noises rose from the yellow house
always on time—the house with the big anchor.

But somebody, *some*time, must have said, "Where are
the Aldriches?" and I hold Gama to blame:

"Hymn-sing, dears, would change our dinnertime.
No, we're not special—simply not the same."

GONE NOW

The lonely apple trees
stood in front of the farmhouse
where the Reardons—our "help"—and their teenage
daughter, Virginia, lived awhile.

There were seven apple trees
all leafy, but no one could eat the fruit,
the hard little apples falling eventually
and having to be picked up.

Driving down to the big house
Dad might remark how
everything looked pretty bleak up here.
I disagreed. For I'd be invited in,

we played the old old records
on the wind-up phonograph that often ran down,
part of the fun, with its big wood handle.
We ate cookies and orange slices.

MY FAVORITE, DEEP-VOICED NEIGHBOR

Little I knew as a kid how drink
and vitriol ran through Harts Neck;
for me the breezes blew, the water was bluer
than Gama's morning glories and balloon flowers.

There was a witty woman who'd joke
with me under a shade tree, and we laughed together.
Years later one night the floorboards broke
after her cigarette and glass dropped and the couch caught fire,

the room caught fire, and she and the furniture
fell cellarward through the smoke smother.
Her humor and her horror. I cannot think
even today of one without the other.

THE GIFT

Gampa died,
and Gama died;
we sold the house.
Where is he
now—
Pinocchio,
who hung
instead of a ring
or tassel
at the end of
the upper-hall-
light string.
For sure,
Gama had loved
and thanked me
often for

this little prize,
Pinocchio,
this 3-inch wooden
figure with
his painted cap
and shoes
and pointed
nose.

BURIAL AT SEA

On a morning sun-struck and still
I rowed out maybe half a mile
with a tight-woven basket of napkin rings.
Among them were Gampa's wide vermilion,
Gama's amber, Mum's thin turquoise,
Dad's metal green with pinks inlaid,
David's and mine we'd no longer need.
I threw them over the water, one
by one, as far as I could.
The others, used by guests I'd known
and liked, I slid over the side.
At first they went down glittering,
then less and less, anonymous.

HERON AT MORNING

"There's that old heron over there," to Nancy
I beckon. The day is half begun with mist.
Why, at that bird's beauty, do I feel so angry?

I sat dumbly at her hospital bed
and never said, never assured her, she
had been a good mother. I thought it went
without saying. Gradually she went without
my saying it. Some pain is permanent.

Three years later they called me down
to the house my parents kept for fifty years.
Our last phone-words had been in argument.
Now, eyes shut, he lay pillowed on the downstairs divan.
Somebody said, "Say something, Jonathan."
I said, "We love you." Didn't quite say "I."
No further word, or inward prayer.
All done. He shivered once and died.

Maybe I never truly spoke gratitude because
I took it all for naturally being there,
like ocean, sky, and rocks—as the bird does.

NIGHT: THE WATER BEARER

Who is that man
between field and river
coattails flapping
skyward at the cold
close of January?
Who is this man
who let the stars
the sky
fold over him.

SONG TO N.

Don't know where I'm goin'
but I know who's goin' with me.
Friends will know already—
it's you, O bonnie Nancy.

We may go back to Eden
although we never met there.
Don't know where we're goin'
and don't know how to get there.

Some say I'm grim,
and some say I'm funny,
but I will ever be
your win some, lose some, Johnny.

TIVOLI

SONG ONE: Get Out of Town

i

Once many years ago
in the good town of Hillsboro,
having wiped out Luigi
and shuffled some others about,
Edward (Ted) Peely, our hero,

might have been feeling gay,
having attained the height
of middle-management on his floor.
Everything here looked bright. Someday
he'd take over the whole store.

All year doing better and better,
or seeming to anyhow,
he had risen from Sales & Accounts
to General Troubleshooter.
But nobody liked him now.

He felt stalled:
his superiors (so-called)
no longer complimented him.
Somehow a gloom overcame him,
a slow unaccountable gloom:

a slow unaccountable gloom
now filtered down out
of the sky to surround
and vex his waking moments,
had even entered his head

at night whenever
he tossed around. The old motto
"Better Ted than dead"
frankly didn't hold water
anymore, if it ever had.

He read books on philosophy,
putting the pulp aside;
took up the viola. And yet he
discovered that all he tried
only increased the gloom inside.

His doctor, a bewhiskered
silly old son-of-a-bitch,
suggested so and so,
some temporary switch?
So finally Ted departed

those many years ago.

ii

But where to visit? Darkness clung
to the leaves and furrowed along
the hills below him when,
packed suitably, he flew
to Heathrow—toss of a coin.

The moment he touched down
in London's swinging town
he saw how the gaiety
of this land, although not his,
conveyed a sense of place.

He loved the openness,
he could hardly keep his mind
off wondering why oh why
limit himself to England
in this sweet new reality?

Often it seemed a dream.
Occasionally, for a while,

to himself he didn't seem real.
It took him awhile to see
that's what he *didn't* seem.

He sped the rail to Cambridge,
punted the Cam, and strolled
up King's Parade and Trinity
until he struck the old
Round Church—an oddity

built with a sort of layercake
tiering, a conical dome
and small cock weathervane
that spun that blustery morning;
inside, a mix of centuries

as if nobody could care.
He rather liked the circular
walls, he began to relish
this little church, the dampish air
of quietness around the Norman pillars

chunky and fat, a stone
triforium of dogtooth carving
in rough diagonals, a window near
the font, of Christ blessing the children.
Suddenly for no reason

he settled on Scandinavia.

iii

Whenever he looks back
on that year, whenever he remembers
the summer of '65
and youth—redolent, open,
easy—he sees one afternoon

and evening in Copenhagen,
and dusk coming in,
the city as it wished to be.
A sandwich on Hambrosgade,
a single beer. And dusk.

Days for wandering long.
He wandered into the Tivoli
Gardens, where Marlene sang
Honeysuckle Rose.
Goodness knows.

Stopped in his tracks. For who
could ignore—not Ted—
this Dietrich woman singing
in a long white gown? Spotlighted
here in the Tivoli Gardens,

this goddess of the deep deep bow?
And while she endearingly
seemed to be struggling through
or beyond her accent, all
that she did was deliberate, magical,

finally the applause
rose up, and cheers and flowers
carried her off and then
continually back onstage to begin
bowing over and over again.

While this went on and on
—the cheers and applause, the reprise
denied that they were calling for—
Ted noticed a girl beside him. She
said her name was Siri.

All joy is involuntary
and new; and Ted began to feel
the absolute enchantment
of the lighted trees, of anything
blown backward, like a melody

that "just can't help it."

iv

They got to talking.
They had strawberries and cream,
a Danish specialty, and sat
outside an hour on the terrace.
They finished with white wine.

Despite a breeze the evening
stayed warm—or it seemed warm.
They danced on a wide platform
and took the high giant wheel
and looked across and beyond

the park. He felt lightness.
She wore a mild perfume.
Her gentle breasts thrust out
under lace, a lace brocade,
her fingers ringless.

She would be going "back
to Sweden in the fall,
to be studying medicine.
I want to *help* people," she said;
"And what do you do yourself?"

"I'm—well—in clothes, the retail
game," he was muttering.

Then he said, "I don't know.
I don't know what I want to do."
He admitted it outright.

And the wheel came slowly down
only to rise again.
The park twinkled below them.
"I study now in Stockholm."
Ted was going there, too,

if somewhat roundaboutedly.
Oh, what do we ever remember
of times so long ago—
of strawberries, music, lace,
and the soft, piecemeal night—

and the next morning's rent-a-car
driving alone through Denmark
northward, so to arrive
perhaps a week later where
the great sea of Jutland lay

gray on a long gray day.

v

Up Norway's
inner eastern coast,
remembering Siri now,
dispirited, Ted drove at last
to the far city of Oslo.

A weird display of forty
years' art work in Frogner Park,
the huge Vigeland sculptures
shot skyward high and phallic.
They were *too* high, really.

"Tossed like a poker chip"
he felt. Whatever this trip
was meant to be doing, it wasn't.
At night he sat and drank
under a leafy crescent.

After much frosty Heineken
he attended half an hour's
Japanese film in Norwegian.
He noted colorful images,
admired the flow and montage

and staggered into the men's room.
A tall foreigner beside him
grabbed Ted quite lovingly
and swung our hero about
too drunk to object or enjoy it.

Traveling fjords, he held up
his telephoto lens
dutifully over water
on water, although his funds
were drying up like his luck.

He knew he could photograph
this scenery much better—
he just didn't care enough.
Frankly, any old fool
could come and *look* if it mattered.

He headed home that week.

SONG TWO: How Little We Know

i

Now we come to a critical
dip in Ted's career, or shall
we call it simply unfortunate,
given his increasingly sour
attitude in the store?

Suddenly his old gambling habit
took over and held sway:
and now to any fellow worker
he might approach and say
"Hey, do you want to bet?"

It became quite irritating,
this betting on anything
like a fly crawling up the wall
or over the sill,
how far it would get,

or whether, say, he himself
could sell a particular hat
to that fussy customer
thumbing through sweater and shirt
displays by the glove shelf.

He'd say, "Do you want to bet?"
and nobody wanted to,
not really—but Ted kept after it,
and what could a person do,
faced with the protocol

of pleasing the "boss"
when suddenly, after all,
Ted had been given the power
(by an old partner, his uncle)
to hire and fire the workforce.

So everyone tended to bet
on everything under the sun,
and the clothing section became a tense
area with often several
bets going at once.

His underlings, in sum,
put forth the required response
by simply indulging his whim,
so despite Ted's occasional humor
and wit and intelligence

people continued to hate him.

ii

Now Saturdays would find
him halfway up the grandstand
perhaps with some misled
pretty young woman he had
or hadn't yet taken to bed.

He'd wear a feathered sports cap
as he sat in the sun there
enjoying the structure and atmosphere
of the fine hot afternoon,
the sky like cotton candy, and then

they'd be trotting out of the paddock
as elegant as could be,
soon to be rounding the bend
in a frolic, making a dust-up,
and it wasn't, of course, for Ted,

a mere matter of winning
but also—and better—to see
young Joyfoot, Handigirl, Bet-Me-Now
(this latter a fine gelding)
all sulkied up and running.

Quite sensibly, like many
a fan, Ted favored a fast track
but stayed informally ready
to give the longshot a crack
if the field was muddy;

for here was the true scenario
he loved, the murmuring buzz
of the infield, and everything "go!"
—though on family days less so,
e.g. the afternoon

one bouncy towhead kid
jumped up and down endlessly
beside him. And we can't admire Ted
for his response here—he
kicked over the kid's Pepsi.

Ted liked to visualize
the overall stance of his rooting
and cheering, not merely
the race, but himself consorting
happily out with his honey,

whoever his honey was.

iii

Perhaps it may surprise
us that, for all his troubles,

not to mention sore
relationships and various
work-related quibbles

and controversies, Ted enjoyed
a generous female following
outside the store;
and though he seldom stayed
the course with anyone for more

than a month or two, much fun was had:
racing, dancing, cinema,
cocktails before dinner,
a wrap-up in his small
apartment typically going well

though sometimes not;
and furthermore, if you
or I have trouble swallowing
this sort of touch-and-go
activity on Ted's part,

remember Ted
was intelligent and canny,
sensitive, a good reader, who would
have attended museums in Hillsboro
had there been any,

who often took
advantage of whatever the culture
offered, and soaked up a lot,
always a man to appreciate
the latest look.

So at the store, on company
credit, he bought swanky furniture.
A girl from the interior

decoration corner dropped over,
but didn't "come through"—

being so attuned, she knew
the old adage: *Never eat
at a place called Mom's, or play
cards with a guy named Doc,
or sleep with someone who's got*

more troubles than you do.

iv

Permit a brief aside.
While Ted made no great forays
into world literature, he did
enjoy a lively read
at bedtime—old detective stories.

And if, along with betting,
his psychological fervor
went into spotting
the single ingenious answer
to a mystery laid bare,

it's to his credit
he never did downplay
those highfalutin literary
critics who couldn't "care
who did it."

Tackling even *The Moonstone*
he found a character who,
when caveats were called for,
would simply riffle open
his copy of *Robinson Crusoe*

and let a finger fall
randomly on some line
or two he'd then apply
to his own personal quandary;
and likewise Ted,

suddenly wanting a similar
oracle of his own
(if lighter and more portable),
devised a color-coded,
octagonal wooden die

that—always after first
writing out his query—he
would carefully throw
and observe the particular color
landing uppermost

and then apply a pre-
determined metaphorical
message to his life. And all
this came from simply
reading *The Moonstone* through

and thinking about it.

v

Still luckier at post,
he won a longshot daily-
double one hot afternoon;
a later trip to Vegas almost
tripled up his fortune.

So why wasn't Ted content,
amassing all this money?
Because his work with shallow
colleagues made his life
a dismal walk-through.

Five times the cycle went
around and the leaves fell;
snow fell and went and came
again, apparently the same snow,
certainly not much different,

until he desired Hillsboro
no longer, but envied the traveler
who feels a moonlit current
of breeze on his cheek
at the train's open window.

"When I heard Marlene sing
in the Tivoli Gardens I knew
we had something,"
he took to reminiscing
through one year's residue.

He didn't mention Siri
to anyone, however.
Often he thought about her.
But he lacked all energy.
All energy. Without her.

"I want to fall asleep
and forget everything I know,"
he badgered Dr. Mayhue.
"Someday you will," said the doctor,
"but until then, try not to."

So in May, with only minor
prep, after finally
five long summers and the length
of five long winters too,
he boarded an ocean liner

to take his journey out.

SONG THREE: Cool Water

i

In vino veritas
as the saying goes, and I suppose
it's true, but as
for manners, liquor made
scant difference in Ted's case,

his flaws being equally genuine
sober or drunk, on display
at dinnertime especially.
Such as taking the last bun—
he'd do that anyway.

Just when we're ready to like
Ted, he does something or other
we wouldn't excuse in our own mother.
Such as calling a female passenger
at his table a "bull dyke."

Granted, he muttered this epithet
under his breath, or rather
let's say he permitted
himself a stage whisper,
but certainly she caught it.

Yes, his flaws were simple and fast
indelicacies mostly,
and occasionally offered merely
in jest, and yet they cost
him dearly.

A gentle noonday breeze.
Time for the cap and shades!
(Forget your Polaroids;
use the opaques that mirror back
the sky and clouds.)

A pleasant enterprise
to wander along "C-deck."
Enjoyable to gaze
at all those sensuous swimmers
who couldn't see his eyes.

Another gambling spell
took him at dusk: the wheel
and blackjack, where a group
of participants lined up
behind him and played

the same, for he did so well.

ii

But after a day out he felt
tired of everything.
Keeping or not keeping
alive was all the same
to him—as "all the sea is salt."

At night, porthole ajar,
he'd hang a weary arm
out to midair, letting his warm
hand feel the complementary
touch of cool air.

Later, waking, he'd see
only waves and horizon and sky
outside the porthole, dawn
coming to life again,
but nothing to make him lively.

Conjuring up a fantastical list
of girls and naked bodies and war
and trumpets, he'd diddle

with himself in bed before
washing up for breakfast.

But soon to relax. To feel the sea
below, and evening air.
At last to hear a small jazz combo
spotlighted on a stage there,
double-bass and piano.

To feel the undertow.
To contemplate the sea-
god's nature. To savor the lyrical
night and personally
unwind, letting a pale

ribbon of sweet drambouie
slide down the tongue, and let
"trouble slip off your shoulder,"
to reconfigure the future
and past with equanimity.

And so he sat
to the combo's "Moon Over Tennessee"
and "Embraceable You," along
with his own signature song
"Everything Happens To Me,"

floating his little ghosts about.

iii

Floating his little ghosts about!
his habit as he sat
alone and didn't need to chat.
Until the interval drifted by,
nothing could equal that.

But soon, because this bar
was small and not,
of course, his own exclusively,
he had to put
all reverie and thought aside

when suddenly a crowd
descended, shouting rowdy
jokes and anecdotes, the mood
competitive—inviting!
and soon he found himself reciting

a litany of false events
and European travel stories
(he'd been abroad himself but once)
unraveling a vivid series,
"and yes," he said,

arriving finally at a true
experience,
"when I heard Marlene sing
in the Tivoli Gardens, I knew
we had something!"

And he added, "I even spied
her smiling at me" to peak
it off. "I headed over to shake
her hand, but got waylaid
by the crowd, so I never did."

A semi-attractive, giggling, fat
young woman who appeared
to be single and wiggled a lot
continued to pressure Ted
for a traveling update.

Ted ordered up another round
for everyone . . . why not?
More anecdotes and stories. . . .
Later the fabric tended, though,
to fray, to fall apart,

without much sound.

iv

The plump one stayed behind
like a lingering thread;
an awkwardness. It became
apparent she wouldn't mind
accompaniment to her stateroom.

Unbuckled, his pants down,
he was encountering
the biggest, sloppiest chest
he'd ever had the pleasure.
She lay back, wanting anything.

He realized beforehand, during,
he'd surely need to avoid
and dodge this girl for the rest
of the voyage afterward,
but he lunged ahead

partially as a favor,
as she herself puffed and heaved
and gagged, caught up as if
she hadn't been satisfied
in years, or perhaps ever,

the joys of the flesh upon
her, she'd closed her hands
around his neck, she must have been
drawing blood in this totally
go-for-broke performance,

as he uttered a foxhole prayer
he wouldn't be sandbagged
if she suddenly tried
to roll over on top of him
for air or whatever—however,

there came a rushing, a flushing as she
cried out, as they both cried out
together in a crazed ecstasy
of some kind, but Ted's
was simply that it was over!

He left her soaking and fled.
He hurried for night air
without goodbye. Whatever slant
we take on Ted, no matter
what slack we give him, we can't

and shouldn't defend him here.

v

I might go on forever.
Actually I'd prefer to
bow out on reciting a few
more episodes that do
our hero no credit whatever.

Better to pull back on
total disclosure.

And anyhow, why squander
my own descriptive knack on
Ted's shipboard behavior?

Indeed, this is the very point
I've dreaded, of losing your sympathies,
as Ted lost all the passengers'.
But if I don't moralize
a bit, certainly Ted won't.

Consider: Is Ted ever there
to open a door for anyone?
Or to pull out a chair?
Not Ted. If anyone calls
for help, he's somewhere else.

Sporting an off-hand air.
If Ted was going through
some vaguely redemptive, last-minute
nostalgia, feel free to imagine it.
Imagine now, if you care to,

a single man leaning
alone at the ship's railing
above a half-lit sea. A flow
of foam. A whitish furrow.
Imagine no

moon or stars. Only a mist
and breeze. Imagine a man
at the ship-edge imagining Siri
herself and even a lost
conversation they never had:

*I could never find you again
afterwards* might run the words.
Or: *You were always leaving me*
he says, almost aloud.
Here you imagine Ted

better than he himself could.

SONG FOUR: These Foolish Things

i

We pick him up today
walking the streets of Bergen
as comfortable and blasé
as if he'd never been
five summers out of Norway.

He felt in the right place.
And the pocket die he carried
everywhere nowadays
(as good luck token) appeared
to be saying likewise.

Let me explain the die.
You pose a serious question
about yourself or the future
and throw the die: the color
on top will signify

the relevant one of eight
responses: *Exactly; Proceed to the gate;
Back off; An excellent query;
Yes!; No!; Hardly a moment
to spare; A worthy bet.* . . .

Often with nothing more
to do at night
he'd throw the die, and once
in drunken haze
he dropped it out the window.

One night by happy chance
he gazed across the courtyard
to another house and spied
two women in pajamas!
Delightful foreigners

all sleepy and alone?
What with his dinnerful of wine
it might have fallen out
the luckiest of pleasures
to scurry on down his own

fire-escape and up theirs,
but knowing this could provoke
an international incident,
he found it better to keep
Siri in mind this trip.

Even his die said so.

ii

A light Norwegian rainfall
had come and gone,
the sky turned bright and colorful
again, and sunny Bergen
now made it suitable

(despite another hangover)
to sit and view
the red-tiled architecture
of slanted roofs and varied trim
and citizens around him,

see the fresh morning market
(although he always thought
of Siri) to where the wharf ran out
displaying fish and reindeer-
skins and flowers and fruit.

By now he had creamed off
the best of Bergen—the tower,
the Hanseatic wharf

museum, the cableway and bus tour,
he'd even hiked enough.

Something for privacy.
And yet at times he felt resentful
sitting alone....
Life was hardly fair!
Life was all balled up. People

had balled *him* up from square
one. And where was the fun
or point of traveling on and on
with nobody to share
his thoughts with, finally?

Today the face of Siri,
her happy eyes, remained
forever as true and clear
and brilliant in his mind
as on that earliest hour

those years ago in Tivoli
when she had laughed and talked
of travel, telling him how,
as long as she found work,
she might go anywhere,

practically anywhere.

iii

So day by day, he saw
great steamers underway
until, well-ticketed, he
sailed up the coastal
fjords of Norway after all.

To Lindås. Florø.
Kristiansund. The fruit trees
blossoming at water's edge.
Trondheim's tall cathedral,
Bodø, Reine, the Lofoten Islands,

Tromsø, the "northern capital,"
while he imagined also
the far interior with trolls
within those snowy mountains,
great shaggy vegetation

spilling from their noses—moss
and bushier juniper
and carrots, even Christmas
trees, per chance, in winter—
their hideous swinging tails

all long and hairy;
and it is said if trolls
encounter sunlight they
explode, becoming the stones of Norway.
He'd almost forgotten Siri

... until his steamer crossed
the 70th parallel
and came to the topmost
city of the whole world's map,
old Hammerfest

and suddenly, at the top
of his long one-nighter,
he saw the midnight sun,
at last that great free-floating
sun bestowing lovely poison

pinks and oranges and slate-gray violets far over
the long wind-ruffled water
to shadowy ice-peaks
on the horizon
like the eye of a great lover

that will not die. . . .

iv & v *The Release*

. . . And now it was like a dream
traveling where the pocket
die directed following
south to Sweden and watching
for Siri   always Siri

Onward a flight to Paris
but the city itself proved
disappointing some people
enjoy the big city some
don't and Ted simply didn't

Gathering wits however
and traveling west to Chartres
as if by some miracle
the sun blazingly appeared
and organ music rumbled

precisely as he entered
and windows oh the great rose
windows gothic arches high
and interior lacework
glowed over nave and transept

yet he discovered no one
familiar here and always

south by railway again when-
ever the waiter brought a
wine list he was into it

Down to a lovely red-clay
village of the Vaucluse got
red dust all over himself
seeing ancient men at boules
under a tree of shadows

and deftly oh so deftly
a few sounds but not many
gentlemen were playing boules
throughout the long afternoon
and yet despite a summer

sun he could feel everything
darken whenever a chance
occurred almost as if he
were losing his eyesight and
later when he would expect

to find a seductive light
brightening Aix-en-Provence
as a gray cloud cover kept
turning the stately presence
of Mont Sainte-Victoire off east

still statelier becoming
a mountain to contemplate
as he drank & drank and yes
it seemed the long shadows must
follow him to Italy

and no one here in Florence
at least no person he had
ever seen before namely

not that particular one
answering her description

In San Gimignano the
passage of winding steps
up around over and lost
you right where you thought you saw
an exit by cobblestones

Reaching the Colosseum
the Pantheon and Sistine
Chapel too dizzy to look
at the Spanish Steps to fall
down fountains the whole Roman

shebang carried a wallop
but nobody here again
among seven syllables
whom Athens couldn't supply
either   or the Cyclades

islands all swirling around
Delos the birth-isle of god
Apollo with Mykonos
shoreline-houses as a wind
flapped decorative laundry

And waters off Paros waved
in blue became white on shore
as he favored another
island he needed to see
of placid terraced hillsides

Olive trees are said to live
forever their roots sunning
underground to poke up here
and there lifting up other
trees still burgeoning where new

olives grow and blacken from
blossoms born a million days
and darkness long ago and more
olives fall to your salad
plate or is it all one tree?

Then gentle a rain appeared
to olive groves and he passed
a tipsy evening after
bread and moussaka and walked
side roads into a moonlit

quarry to find the famous
stone   the Venus de Milo
once fashioned from this very
marble so glimmering here
and white to last forever

tonight all shadowy but
he saw there in the moonlight
well enough to roll the die
and ask *Is my trip over
now should I be going home. . . ?*

and the die said

Exactly

SONG FIVE: Honeysuckle Rose . . .

i

I want to thank you, reader
(assuming you're still here), for how
you've tolerated Ted, while I
myself am growing rather
sick of him by now.

Did Europe make him better?
What lesson could he learn, or what
bring back in thought or insight?
Less than the average traveler
might! No matter,

but giving him every break
after such long exposure
to criticism, I'd like
to bring his story to closure
for everybody's sake.

It was the best season
to return—new buds and trees
were scented or moving on,
everything wore the fair
glance of spring, tulips and crocuses

taking their color
that typically came late
to Hillsboro and, that very year,
had been delayed by drought
and chilly weather.

Old-timers in the store,
wondering what to expect
and resenting the cavalier
way Ted often had wrecked
relationships before,

took a deep breath
against the expected schism
so liable to come
and waited, waited. Yet both
his tone and rhythm

of voice implied a subtle
shift, as if some private myth
or meaning he had brought back with him
made Ted a little
easier to get along with,

though not much easier.

ii

And if in the first year
he half-expected to see her
stepping around a corner
or lunching below an umbrella,
let's say, at Pierre's outdoor

café in May; or if he
half-caught, it seemed, her bright blonde
hair, a shoe, a similar
tilt of shoulders, or the hand
he had held so briefly,

"I won't tell anyone,"
and "I am insane," he thought,
remembering always, or little
by little again, the lights
and warm air, his own

happiness when even by day
occasionally, as the mood
would soften, some little arc

of existence carried him back,
although still profitless

to wonder why oh why
a trick of dusk truly became
Siri—Siri again—her kindness
and beauty she had shown him,
her desire to help others.

And yes, of the famous Dietrich
singing a song or two
in a beam of light, he would speak
openly of her in the few
times he had gone public

on the joys of Copenhagen
but never, however, a word
about Siri; and when
he thought, as he often did,
"I am crazy—insane,"

why was he any crazier
than the great Dante, say, who saw
a simple schoolgirl once
one single afternoon somewhere
along a street in Florence

and made an epic of her?

iii

Ted began to write songs.
He wrote in the popular style
although his songs weren't popular
at all, for he'd squirrel
them away in a drawer.

Had Ted a hidden reservoir
of talent? No. But his songs
were songs only for Siri, they were
quodlibets of the beautiful things
he had seen, looking for her.

But as he wrote and saw
himself in contrast,
saw that he was impure
and pointless, dull, depressed
and silly compared to her,

and, worse—it became worse—
competitive, smug, greedy,
his life a total foolishness
from the beginning—he
went back and forth on this.

Where did it all go wrong!
Yesterday? Last year?
In youth? or maybe a very long
time ago? in the darkness
of Santa's stocking?

And why, if she did appear
on his doorstep,
would Siri (or anyone) care
to continue or take up
life with him anywhere?

Who would possibly grieve
if he disappeared?
Or care? He became, I would have
to say, quietly near tears,
without beauty, without love.

He began to repair. He put
flowers on his parents' grave.
He tried to behave. And as for
Siri herself to appear,
although his hope seemed hopeless,

he'd give it another year.

iv

Oh, do we all know
a day when our very best
happiness—far away, but calling
and calling to be recovered—
slips or crawls into our head

like an old song that won't go?
So Ted himself was tossed
and swept along
so very far away and lost
and buffeted on a long

nightwind, where mocking people
laughed, it was all he could do
to recall the honestly open
warmth of Copenhagen,
remembering when

all nature lay beautiful
—as if, in his whole
existence, he had been decent
only that single afternoon
and evening, it seemed now

in memory, a brilliance
once like a birthright drifting

away and Siri his only
goodness; and wasn't there any
way (insane as he was!)

to keep her, to see her again?
"Her face always before me,"
but vaguer and disembodied
as a distant voice is,
forever telling him not

to forget, as if he owed
Siri a debt.
Of course he could not foresee
the future, another decade
to come, the old glory

of songs and singers dead
or dying away—even the snarly
Marlene holed up in her Paris
apartment going to pieces—
his own lifetime ahead.

But that is another story.

v

It is over at last.
Now in early December
of 1974
he has taken to a side-
street pub in Hillsboro

cozy Hillsboro
to hear an incongruously
young piano
player playing the old ones.
What does a young man know?

"Whatever's over is past,"
as he finishes up his Bud
and neon comes on outside.
There has been a light snow
and more is forecast.

Almost ready to go
he thinks to himself now:
"So if the future is hard
I can think of my earlier
luck, what luck I've had."

Tonight is merely the first
night he will entertain
a gathering gratitude.
Somehow the future deepens
for people all at once.

The melody is slow
and quick and offhand by turns,
but suddenly he feels no
unhappiness—only an odd
nostalgia as the pianist

tries "Honeysuckle Rose."
For it is over, he knows
she is gone, she will never
appear anywhere again
except in dreams . . . not ever. . . .

Years later Ted became good.
Nobody understood.
"It wasn't of course Marlene
but Siri—my knowing her
once in the Tivoli Gardens,

in the wonderful Tivoli Gardens."

OWED TO *FINNEGANS WAKE*

for my children

Note:

On certain Sundays when my brother and I were young, our father would read aloud a short passage or two from Joyce's last great work. He never stumbled, the words sounded wonderful, and his readings left me with a fascination for the incomprehensible. Last winter, five years after my father's death, I managed to read (or pass my eyes over) the entire "novel," making eclectic responses as I went along. I hope a tolerance for some obscurity may exist in my readers, too.
    —J.A.

i.

        F

alls   away a   up in dreams
  the   shut   night-   open
    common world   world to
      day-   teems

ii. *I am*

too old to be Sir Tristram
fr'over the short sea,
no, I am not Sir Tristram
nor was meant to be,

he rumored to be wooing
in some far countree.
One wonders how he's doing
over the short sea!

It won't be long now,
a star said, and forsaking
others, Sir Tristram now
forever will be pecking,

shooting, looting.
My, oh my!
Here he comes parachuting
out of a blue sky!

iii. *pundit*

Lofty Humpty high on a wall
knows passing cloudlets, blah blah blah.
Down one side he spots the limber
Liffey glinting through appletime.
Down the other, if he did a 180,
he'd view the shadowshards of himself.
Beware a thunderclap, Egghead!

iv. *tavernbanter*

As I staggered home off Eccles Street one night I thought I heard:

—Who cares about *Head-in-Clouds* who walked the earth?

—Buddha nother pint of brew . . . .

—Uh?

—Would argue he weren't entirely sexual at it, Wicky, ha! ha!

—Thank guinness, lad. For auld lang sin, drink up. . . Another quark for my friend, here.

—Drink up, let's we forget.

—Let's we forget, me lad, drink up!

v. *family fugue*

HCE and Anna Livia
bequeathed us children three:
Shaun the postman, Shem the penman,
and protean Issy.

But something shameful in the Park
was done by HCE.
And Anna Livia meandered into
the scrotumtightening sea.

vi. *so please the court*

What shall we sing of Phoenix Park?
That after spring and summer hours
and maybe a fugitive touch of rime
the ground will rise again in flowers?
That like the park in the movie *Blow-Up*
(its origin a different crime)
we're always a tad from the truth, even ours?
And who doesn't love the rustle of leaves
to the wind's swirl in the treetops there?
Who but the law will mind if, hidden
in bushes, dallies a scurvy bud?

vii. *the children's dance*

Lucifer flies from flower to flower
to the lilt of guessing games and colors
of children neither his nor ours.

See them dancing hand-in-each
round hazel, cedar, oak, elm, peach

in a tumble bounce of their own drum,
trouncing the devil thrice, then home
to prayers and the nod of sleep. Mummum

(music: Tom Aldrich)

viii. *the lessons chapter*

> *"You might bloom, Jonathan, if you only tried."*
> —Miss Galt

No, really I cannot blame
those lovables, little Issy
and Shaun and Shem,
for wanting to skip the essay.

In childhood I myself was glad
to critique rather than "bloom."
In Painting Class, after a dab
or two, I'd wander the room

and pinpoint the fault
occurring or about to occur
on every sheet. Miss Galt,
though irked, was bound to concur.

Miss Babcock taught mathematics,
Dr. Applegate self-reliance
(his method just a bag of tricks),
Miss Brill the great dilemmas of science:

how the small laws work for the small,
big laws work for the big,
but neither works for the other at all!
I didn't give a fig.

Somehow these teachers got me by.
And while they acquiesced
it is Miss Galt's suggestion I
"might bloom" that I remember best.

ix. *pauper's debut*

If Shem the penman mixes piss
and poop for ink, remember this:

from stinking mud rises the cool lotus.

x. *the washerwomen*

Tree and stone
will sing as one.
The run-off sings adieu.

Dusk is coming,
nightshift humming.
Wring out the clothes! Wring in the dew!

xi. *out of the woods*

Why is it such fun to read about poisons?
Take simply fragile fungi, for example.
Of these, see first the Amanita family.
The Death Cap, or Amanita mutabilis,
sports reddish capsules that smell rather like anise.
Though not as dangerous as some, there's no known antidote.
(Perhaps a liver transplant?)

Turn for worse effect to the Cortinarius family.
The Deadly Web (ovellanus, or rubellus) acts so
clandestinely that symptoms may not peak for weeks—
with eventual renal failure!
Likewise the Galerina (autumnalis, marginata, venenata).
Keep watch also for fiber heads (Caesar's f., tom f., and scaly f.).
Other noteworthies:
Psilocybe semilanceata,
Copirinus atramentarius,
Teonanacatl,
Gyomitra infula.
Ah yes, what fun!
For curatives, see your doctor when you can.

xii. *home funeral*

Bob had taken a stress pill
and looked unduly cheerful.

Goldilocks
was thinking outside the box.

Harry hadn't for years
seen such sparkling food and tears.

Hams, turkeys, salads, wine, whiskey, cheeses
and sweets and other surprises.

Whoever you are, looking so lovely and true,
don't wake up, we love you!

xiii. *sibling twins*

Shem and Shaun, rivals in youth,
are gone together. Both!
(And certain other folk, who were
cantankerous with death.)

But dance a jig for Ireland if
they ever made you laugh.
'Tis better to be jolly, sir,
than lead a life o'wrath.

xiv. *lovers*

Heaven looked in, along with those less godly,
and all the birds of the sea when it was dark,

blown plover, curlew, kestrel—and four landsmen
unblinkingly. So from the Bigbang of

Creation down to the 15-inch loveseat,
carry the good news: Love never dies!

Nobody else has known love's high shenanigans
better than this pair. Amen! Amen!

And may their loving live forever even
when they have flown, like yesterday's weather.

xv. *siglia*

My easiest sleeps came in a fourposter,
a pencilpoint bed, inherited,
without curtain, canopy or lace,
having no barrier.

Nightly my eyes drew triangles,
right-angled arcs, a rectangle
with the carved tips
invoking kindred spirits.

xvi. *transactiondentation*

Ugh! Ugh! A bug crawled out
of my ear last night, and when I stirred
in bed to distinguish dream
from other realities, I heard

the Word

of words—my yet unwritten
soul that cried the casting
of bread and wine on the Water
of waters is everlasting.

xvii.

tell

me all about

Anna Livia! I want to hear

\-

\-\-\-\-\-\-\-\-\-\-\-\-\-\-\-\-\-

ALL-

xviii. *the toy fair*

My father carried me along
as far as he could
          then set me down
beside him in a ferriswheelchair

and up and down we went
up and down
up and down
up and down
in the night air

xix. *in my end is my beginning*
(T.S. Eliot)

As I near the close of what many a soul
has thought a yawning book
sheer baubles of babytalk
God knows how many indolent hours
of mine have gone somewhere
have flown somewhere
and shall I try it all again
Shall oranges be laid to rust
on the green again
As the pages blow and turn oh let a last one cling
    to my finger
and hoops of childhood flare
yes yes I am small again

xx. CODA

times and spaces

    snow is general

        cover the pages

over Ireland

    gulls are calling

        river rises

pluck out his eyes

    a world collected

        rejoycing always

GENERATION

i

W thought he was
his own son, young w.
What's going on?

He sent young w to Spain
when the occasion arose.
He imagined a rose

in the hair of young w_2
if she could be found there.
He would pay

for the rose
one way or another—please.
O please be ours

he'd say,
if occasion arose.

ii

The characters may speak
as the curtain rises.
Los personajes. . . . Action
begins in midstream anyway,
the audience catching up
as it listens. . . . *Los personajes,
los personajes.* . . . A play
should have a theme we can
state simply;
eight minutes in,
an audience should feel
the direction of things
and the probable outcome.
Los personajes pueden hablar. . . .

iii

Young w sat comfortably on a
veranda in Sevilla
remarking the senoritas.

As he wrote to his father:

*Estoy cansado ahora, pero
!que milagro estar
aqui¡ Son los siete y ya
hace mucho calor.* . . .

But how little his father
knew of the colors and culture
of Andalusia—
essentially *nada!*
Moreover, this letter will send old papa
to *el dictionario* ha ha.

iv

As editor-in-chief of *The Daily Sun*
W put much on his son w, for w was the only one.

He wanted w to shine,
and had many thoughts and notions along this line.

Sometimes he wondered if w was a pansy because
    the boy didn't date around town,
but he knew this couldn't be true and basically he wanted w
    to marry and settle down.

After all, W himself was getting older.
But w spent much of his time taking photographs
    and putting them in a folder.

Perhaps the boy could turn his photographic skills
    to advantage? one could always use
some attractive travel pictorials in the Sunday
    supplement instead of news.

W loved to chat with his son, he knew
there was something special between the two,

yet always, after a spell of banter and lingering quiet spells,
they fell quiet as sea shells.

v

In the *Plaza des los Venerables*
w cut a fortunate deal
and looked down on orange trees in a small
rectangle diagonally cobblestoned,
where two *restaurantes* set their white
and dark green tablecloths and wooden chairs,
and the windows were lacy-iron scrolled
(so no one could get in and steal?)
and lanterns hung above the windows, red
flowers on windowsills, at night
a guitarist plucking out
some Andalusian folksong w recalled
from an old French movie long ago.
Near sleep, from not afar, he heard the great cathedral bell.

vi

Clouds hung over the dull
metropolis where W
ran his newspaper.
Perhaps he'd never really
said enough to w
on how to live!—always
his impetus would cool,
cool as the rain
that rains "on the just
and the unjust fella.
Except the unjust fella
doesn't get wet
because he stole
the just's umbrella."

vii

So w let the days drift by
in Sevilla, fate lifting over the river
Guadalquivir each day like sunrise
just as the sun rose high
and dreamlike over *el rio Guadalquivir*
a beauty would mystify, lie
deep in the brown bones of Sevilla
below the decorative squares
and narrow alleyways,
the minarets and pilasters
of black filigree, the orange trees
and warm *barandas* and flowerpots,
the glazing white-
washed houses, the white doves.

viii

W had hoped his son would find
a livelihood
in Sevilla.

La la la, a new
attitude
in Sevilla from what he left behind.

But his son was only dancing
and eating food
and drinking wine in Sevilla.

Wasting the time of day and up to
no good
in Sevilla.

Ever the same old kid—
robbing him blind!

ix

Certainly when w had flown to Spain
it seemed the right thing.
W had watched the plane pulling away
at 10:02—then back to the old office.
Okay, you tally up pros
and cons and make a choice.
"So we said goodbye to the boy, he's on
assignment," said W, covering.

Evening. After a bath and martinis
he drew out his Rand McNally atlas
and measured the water between here and Spain:
3 ½ inches. Oh yes, he'd found that atlas
on remainder, "cheap at half the price"
as the joke goes, he remembered the day. . . .

x

Once they'd spent a lovely time
together long ago—a run
of classic film noir in the living room,
a bluish flicker filling the room
with nightly old-time murder movies,
Double Indemnity for one,
the quintessence of deception . . . like the time
when Fred MacMurray arrives and a neighborly song
is drifting through her window . . . "Tangerine . . ."
her eyes of green. If you knew the song
you knew the answer, and W sang to the movie:

"Oh she's got the boys on the run,
But her heart belongs to just one,
Her heart belongs to Tangerine. . . ."

xi

Down to the darkened
evergreen and firs and rocky shore

of New England far
across the warm edge of Spain

(as an early sunlight
over Barcelona moves to warm

the western sector)
W is dreaming and w is dreaming,

and tied to the earth's
turning and the water between them

W deepens and w again
is stirring without knowing where he is.

Where, after all, is anyone on a
single planet in this universe of many?

xii

If w dreams in the dark a.m.
he wakes to remember
repartee, some watery flow
of images without
much color—more
like the old film noir
he had shared with his father
long ago—but now each dream
unreeling either
clear scenes mysteriously
connected or
mysterious scenes
connected clearly. What
should he prefer?

xiii

No one can know
the color of the sea,
if it is turquoise
gray or green or blue
or only colorless
at heart,
seeing it vary
so above.
No one can say
exactly why
it varies so,
or how,
or what it is a
variation of.

xiv

As w went riffling through literature-cum-translations
of the country he found

Nasin cand' as prantas nasen,
No mas des froles nasin....

by Rosalina de Castro, writing in her nineteenth
century verse of Galicia up northwest:

I was born when plants were born, / in the month of
flowers I was born, / on a dawn soft and gentle, /
    on an April dawn.

But where, for w, is that lady of olives under the wide
blue skies of Andalusia, where is she?

As if the roses ... or not ... the roses? ... thus
and thus

until, to a toe-tapping scenario, an evening comes for
w and, with it, love.

XV

Curtain up! and flashily
here in the spotlight
half a dozen young flamenco
dancers stomping to guitars and dizzy
castanets go dancing round
and snapping castanets, all bright
in color, costume, swish of thigh and toes,
the *cante chico* and *soleares*
leaping loose and tight
and energetic as a bullfight,
while of the pretty dancing girls
one in particular brought to mind
the unnecessity of all this noise,
and yet—and yet—

xvi

—after the interval
watching this girl, he
felt the lingering wingbeat
of an underthought
until a gathering answer
hit him all at once:
of making for his father's *Daily Sun*
(to satisfy his father)
a photographic layout—yes,
of the full flamenco scene in Andalusia
focusing on the life and dance
and aspirations of a single dancer
(call her w_2)! And so his fate:
to go backstage and ask.

xvii

And she agreed!
And now he saw how a land's
beauty with a girl's beauty blends.
Workdays went by, went by,
went by, click of the shutter,
click of the shutter, no raincloud
in the future, text and photos
lined his walls until he had
the "who, what, where, when, why"
that newspapers impose,
he had it all, but w
sent nothing to his father
as he and w_2
became close.

xviii

In their ritual time
together high
in his room midday
(the blinds half-drawn
in the midday heat)
how easily over
and over the lips
of her mouth to the lips
of her thighs O! the peppery
scent of her skin
awakens over
and over and finally
spent they lie as the
orange trees below them ripen O!

xix

Back home, W felt an inclination
to sit and smoke on the back porch one evening.
Christ, I got you over there. So make it pay!
Tonight he'd put the Sunday edition to bed,
a fine religious spread. Now he noticed,
before he lit his briar pipe and blew
smoke rings up, how an odor of phlox or something
perfectly sweet rose from his neighbor's garden.

Perhaps he might have liked to walk in that garden
idly, say, like a bodhisattva under
this drifting sky. Tonight, if he could bounce
one idea from a star to w, he'd say
Listen, my boy, my boy, we CHOOSE
to fail or to take responsibility.

xx

w and w$_2$ are like one lover
strolling the intimate loops and bends
of the old barrio back of the river
(not to encounter Carlos or the friends
of Carlos) forever side by side,
and w$_2$ preferring these anonymous
loops and bends (not having quite untied
herself from the fiery Carlos)

and happy under the touch of w's caring,
happy under his touch, the weather
mild and the light varying
in early October so. Not yet a mother
she loves to walk with w, carrying
his child inside her from one turn to another.

xxi

Another languid night. Warmer. Alone
but never lonely now, w
(nearly home to his *Plaza des los Venerables*)
saw in a far corner

a shadow change as anything
can change, or not, whatever, the knife
went into him as into a watermelon.
He heard a rushing

intake of oceans gathering suck of ocean
waters joining one
to another again as they
have always done, and farther off

could see himself gone falling
falling from the—

xxii

It is another day, another year gone
by—or more than a year since w
had died.

(Like waters moving, everything happens
and flows on.)

Home in America old W has taken the
baby gently from Angelica—his ancient
housemaid—for a moment: the baby,
as ever, watches curiously.

W says nothing although he smiles—
feeling even he's returning a smile.

It is on nights like this he looks down
at the small child in his arms and
into her dark eyes.

NEW AND SELECTED

CHRISTMAS LETTER

Suddenly the childless couples
I knew have children heading for college.
A baby I knew is taking a wife.
The poems I memorized in youth
are gone. It's time to change my life.

No one has learned to live snugly.
Too many wars and hurricanes
and corruption in high places.
Much lower down, my cards at bridge
are ludicrous: no kings or aces.

And yet what makes this happiness
I feel when I survey my wife
and home and children and a Sunday
snow falling like meditation?
Finally who can say what grace is?

THE CARRIAGE MAN

It's springtime. I have taken four
couples around in the past hour.

My carriage is older than it was.
I have to worry about the doors.

I worry about the seats in general,
cracked leather, worn material.

My horse, for all you think of her
willingness, is an amateur.

And yet the course we take is strewn
with crimson, yellow, purple, green.

OUR WESTIE, ROBERT

When finally we had to put Robert away
I was in the 12th grade reading *The Odyssey*.
Do people really like reading *The Odyssey*?
It makes me want to travel and not travel.
But at the end you get a change of heart.
While one suitor after another suitor woos
Penelope, who must be *very attractive!*
and says she won't put out till her weaving is done
and cleverly unravels some each night,
The Great Traveler suddenly gets to her doorstep!
(It's hard to remember why he left in the first place—
oh yes, the War) and the little dog
jumps all over him. It left me feeling
everyone is looking for each other.

THE BIRD OF PARADISE
(for Veronica Benning)

Although I can't remember the place,
it landed, looked at me, took off,
colors flared like a pinwheel or sparkler
or a beach umbrella twirling in the wind.
What feathers—what color and grace!
I had been thinking till then
it was always a flower—that seemed enough—
but firstly of course it's a real bird,
this Bird of Paradise.

Yet all is not well. Although
the colors we love are real, and wind is real,
the sun, the island sands are real, the injuries
our children and others bear and never truly talk to us about
are real and always will be,
"Life is a disease whose only cure is death,"
Freud said without smiling, his little car
speeding across Europe, abjectly colorless.

I, too, have tried to find again
that Bird of Paradise—through memories once:
my baby brother finally quiet in his bassinet
books in the library of our home, our first home, some volumes
    leather-bound, thin pages and gold leaf
an afternoon's thunderstorm pulling away and seeming to
    draw the forest after it
the fence at Bendy's house and snow on the picket tips melting
years later in woods the flattering shudder
Berryman, lively and drunk, dancing at midnight at Bread Loaf
the growing question
those wrong but rightful deaths—tears for
my grandparents
my mother and father
friends
loss oh loss
and where, I ask, is the rose-apple tree I once sat under
    by the Shaker graveyard

and felt joy, wondering what high pursuits
　　　I would be dealt?

So have we all traveled anywhere on earth
to find those colors—New Guinea,
Africa, Ireland, Greece—
whatever the time or cost.
Is the only bird of paradise
the one we lost?

You ask: *Did I hallucinate?*

Ah, no. No, that is not your fate,
and nobody need wait.
Think of all you've done and felt and seen and heard.
The light is white. You have that bird.

THE CONSTELLATIONS ARE NOT FIXED

Oh put an end to wars,
he mused—a kind of prayer

as a dawn-snow fell like gauze.
Tonight, however, is clear

and the indolence of stars
is less than would appear—

Remember: the stars we gaze
at are no longer there.

SOLDIER POET

Let me stay below the olive grove
for England, England always. If you are fool
enough to want to follow, then lie down
and rest awhile among the olive trees.
You may find the air lighter than you think
and the sky broken by little leaves and olives,
many, many twigs of leaves and olives.
You will not stay among the olive trees
but shall get up and wander listlessly
wondering how I went and why, as time
returns from black to blue to yellow again
and the trees blossom handsomely except
on days when breezes carry something back,
an apparition that will not be me.

THE BLOT

Hermann Rorschach (1884-1922) was the son of a painter. He began his clinical studies inspired by Justinius Kerner's *Klecksographien*, a nightmarish collection of notes and visual images that ironically (considering Kerner's suicide) had given rise to a popular, lighthearted game that we see being played by young Hermann and a student friend, Konrad, who also came to enter psychology. When Rorschach died as a relatively young man, his unfinished theories were taken up by various schools in directions that, by the evidence, he would not have intended. The poem begins with my (the writer's) imagining young Hermann in bed at night.

I

Later he must have thought
something twittered at the night window,
briefly discernible like a rustle
becoming itself, it whirred and rested
on the windowsill, jubilant, moonlit,
whatever it was, a folded greeting
with purposes it yet declined
to say fully, some hazily huddled
apparition in the Zurich night.

        And these
blossoms falling? From the trees?
I left off wanting to know
an answer decades ago
whether we had bats or blossoms
tucked to our sycamore limbs
as night came on.

II

In darkness did he get up
and reach his hand to the small spirit there?
Something may have moved or spoken.
A confrontation? a quirk of breeze
under the quaint tassel? phenomena
a boy could take for token joy
on such a night, as childhood closes,
and lie dreaming of a journey equal
to the beauty of his father's paintings?

      But why
   do I speculate when I can simply *say* it was—
   and make it just as real as
   the darkening air we move through,
   the lost puddles, spring, new
   buds we had forgotten?

III

In a corner of the classroom at breaks
Hermann and Konrad are playing *Klecksographien*.
Little Hermann and Konrad are laughing today.
Somewhere a tall teacher watches where
formal curtains hang light in the spring sun.
It will be years before Kerner's sad book
of blots and verses that he left behind,
of ghosts and monsters, after his wife died
and he died, will flutter open.

        And what game
    did I play—the name?
    It may have been Jackstraws,
    pulling a long stick loose
    without budging another,
    even the slightest quiver
    and you were gone.

IV

So he became a serious
handsome man who set ten shapes
for our speculations and died too early.
Then everything changed: he had intended
statistical elements—how *many*
answers; details or the whole picture;
kinetic or still; and so on—not
for us to invite ourselves
or a lost part of ourselves inside,

        and yet
    after his death,
    others began to flow
    into his images, or seemed to,
    releasing here or there
    something to know of light
    and dark and longing.

THE MOTHER

I got my *anima* when small
from one no longer here at all.
She sang some pretty songs to me
and showed me sensitivity
and love for art and artistry—
though later gave me growing pains
by writing books on William James,
away so much it was my curse
to have a dedicated nurse
I didn't relish playing with.
The house felt empty as a sieve
until those writing years were done
and I became the favored one.
A joy it was! And when someone
asked at the door, "Is Mummy in,
my boy?" apparently I said,
"Yes, now that William James is dead."
Today I realize much is gone,
that she won't possibly return,
but when I feel it's all uphill
I can remember in her will
she left me optimistic books.
Philosophy's sweeter than it looks.

CHILD POET

You start along the road *trying to keep
your sanity,* although at that age
you don't know there's any problem.
You jump an oval mud puddle.
There's a cloudless sky, with nothing reflected
in the puddle but a few side maples
and also your legs, of course, passing over.
Lazy cows in the far field are mooing.
Where is everyone this summer morning?
Who cares? There's no particular need.

One day you come to a bridge and stop
on the bridge to look down into the brook
that's moving dully. You see your shape leaning
partly over the bridge, and there's your face
reflected correctly except for the moving current.
You turn your head to the left, then to the right.
One profile is better than the other.
You have been called "cute" many times.
This is a very old bridge—an ancient one
and handsome too. It has no railing.

Trying to keep your sanity
late one summer night in bed
you begin "The Turn of the Screw."
Past bedtime. Little do you know
your father stands on the lawn and sees
a glow under your window shade,
having turned off every electrical thing
in the house and found the meter running.
He comes upstairs and takes the book
away without a word.

Your mother is a good person but
she is not strong enough to stop
the little boy who looks like you
from appearing behind oak trees.

Rarely does the boy try maples—the oak
being his specialty, where he beckons
from boughs and is gone deftly
as you approach—he stays away!

He is no smiler, but seems to be
enjoying himself *trying to keep his*. . . .
And now you hear him rustling bushes
or see a quick hand drawn back. The wind,
especially in this summer dusk, is
trying to keep—well, it blusters
from bush to bush more than looks natural.
It won't help to dawdle, to dawdle
on the pathway up to supper, and yet
he seems your friend, it's best to acknowledge
this presence and accept his care,
or else he may appear anywhere.

Oh, he's better than you—you have
decided this. Sometimes he is standing
at the fringe of a field, *trying to*. . . .
Such hide-and-seek appearances!
At home, before you act or answer,
you imagine, you always think of, this little one.
Nowadays, even while chatting, you
adjust your words, hearing his own words first.
Is he beside you and singing? It seems so.
Yet often he slips away.

Today the air is oddly inactive
in spots, gusty in others, and the cloudy
sun feels neither weak nor strong.
But you know he is bounding along
in groundcover ahead as you walk down
to the brook, *trying . . . trying*. . . . Only sharp
greenery and a bush by the brook

are stirring. No one can keep you from him.
You leap into the feral bush
where there may be song.

ALL POETS LOVE THUNDERSTORMS
(Auden)

It took awhile to know
why thunder and lightning drew me.

Our sunny days were so-so.
But when fall nights got gloomy

I'd stand by a rattling window
glad that nobody knew me

and praying for rains to blow
a dangerous new world through me.

MY FATHER'S PROPHECY (1914)

Running ahead of them to pick
a picnic spot on the island he saw . . . the shell!
Perfect, he thought, despite the nicks and crack
at the mouth; it looked mother-of-pearl.
He held it to his ear. . . . Nothing at all
except the sounds he had already heard.

That summer, though, the shell sat by his bed
on the table, a treasure there.

God! He woke from a nightmare of bombs
and lay there motionless and scared.
Then reaching out, he put the shell to his ear
and heard a far cacophony
that surely wasn't the room's—
it seemed beyond the wish-wash of the sea.

OF UNKNOWING

But who knows anything?
Knowing a little might
be better, of course, than nothing.
Or maybe not.

The other day I bought
a plane geometry
hardback in a dusty bookstore
for something to read

at night if I woke too soon
or couldn't drop off,
the good old ways of axiom,
postulate, theorem, proof,

but found I only
believe these many figures
for the sake of their beauty,
like a childhood memory, say,

of how along a country road
our family would go
to pick grapes for jelly
many years ago now.

ARS POETICA

a.

Archibald MacLeish says "A poem
should not mean / But be."
He says it in a poem, though,
so he can't mean it.

b.

Dr. Johnson says if you write
a line and especially like it,
Sir, strike it.
So I've left out the best part of this poem.

c. *(thinking of those who reject someone's art
because of the kind of person the artist was)*

It never works the other way around.
Nobody says, "Because his private life
was terrific, I love these lousy little poems."

d.

Soon I found myself wandering in graveyards, but couldn't find
    anyone who shouldn't be there.
Yet is it fair
that Ortega, Lorca, Frost, Williams, Eliot, Forster, Tolstoy,
    or even Baudelaire
should have the final say
in what art is? Or the French elite
who say the perfect poem is a blank sheet?

ON FORM

The villanelle's a tricky form of verse!
Read twice, Elizabeth Bishop's seems the worse
for wear. Though clever Dylan Thomas's, of course,
is fabulous, I can't approve the premise
(except maybe as vehicle to nurse
his dying father to be more vigorous).
But Roethke's villanelle is fast and loose
and beautiful. It pivots into space.

BELIEF

Our somber host at table asked us what
was uppermost in our hearts now,
and every one of us must answer, but
I lied. I said it was a cow.

A cow with a copper bell, two fields below
our rented English cottage, slow
and lowing. When I said it, it was so.
Now I'll forever love this cow.

WHITESTONE POND

By legend Percy Bysshe sailed his boats here,
and probably he did when the wind was right.
In those days Hampstead had "a perfect air,"
and during our honeymoon we loved the white
puff clouds reflecting in the pond.
I hadn't read much Shelley—nor have I yet
read much of his work beyond
a few old chestnuts and the famous Ode.
If Winter comes, can Spring be far behind?
has naturally stayed
with me—a perfect line—over the years.
And though we may never go back to Hampstead
I easily imagine Whitestone Pond, the blowing trees
on the Heath, happiness as it was.

MEXICAN ARABESQUE

If, at dawn, I leave you in bed
I step on something beyond dream:
an old, hand-woven rug containing
the force and tenderness of that white-
haired, deep-lined Mexican
who made it for us and then died
weeks later on the straw of his tent.

We like its once blood-red medallion
a calmer, easy gray to the border.
We liked his face, the man who made it.
Now the colorful tints have faded—
but not the errant thread to the edge
to let the soul run in and out
and humble so the weave's perfection.

WEDDING POEM FOR MEGAN AND PETER
(September 13, 2014)

She's so mysteriously kind he can
believe they'll always be together,
bring children into the world, banter
and laugh as years go by, even when
newer couples have begun to splinter.
And if the world goes ever cynical
and dangerous and we can feel
a dark meridian across the water
where others suffer in disease and hunger,
let them grow lovingly, Peter and Megan,
remembering what they must have told each other
one gusty night, as they continue on
doing such simple things as write a letter
or set a rose on the table in the sun.

THE STORKS OF EDAM

This is the best but last day of visiting our son and his wife
    in the Netherlands.
Our rent-a-car passes indolent turf where tulips will bloom later
    in warm weather.
We stop, as a half-finale, in the village of Edam, the windows
    blank, shops shut, no one about.
There's a squawking of invisible birds.
We walk along a small slow-moving canal to see—possibly—
    the square that will sport a summer festival of cheese.
Briskly before us, our son and daughter-in-law, handsome,
    childless, holding gloved hands, look happy.
I, too, feel happy but almost childless, our son a grown man
    and rising musician.
Beside me, from a tall tree, a shaggy-feathered bird I take for a
    stork swoops and glides to the far side of the canal—before
    returning.
No one has spotted him but me.
Now I notice great groups of gathered sticks like burrs in the trees
    and a few watching bird heads.
The cool sun is falling as we return along the dark canal; a barely
    perceptible mist has come.
I see the same stork sitting, embedded in a tangled tree; ahead,
    bare branches, clotted nests against the sky.

PLACES IN MIND

i. In Evora, Portugal

The shadows lengthen. Pots and pans
that glittered on the street are gone.
Father and son have taken hands.
The traffic slows all over town.

ii. Seasonal

Curtail curtains, shun shades,
love the light as fall fades.

iii. Death Piece

We took to strolling the old
district. In Prague
the Jewish graveyard, we're told,
goes generations deep
layered in slabs and shards.
And who takes care
of it? I see tucked in crevices
small notes and prayers,
stones toppled like playing cards.

iv. Entropy

She touches everything.
She touches you and me, the day,
the shiny railroad tracks with rust
and then the rust.

But do not say the future may
be all disorder—all of it—
until you must.

v. Childhood's End

The last bright animal
steps out of the wall

vi. Resolution

He hopes before he dies
to speak with his heart and not his mind,
like something found he had left behind.

vii. From the Beach

Because you are coming home to me today
the stripe of a luckystone runs through the sky.

NERVOUS

Miss Perkins, "lady of the bones,"
came weekly with her diagrams
and pointer and left-over bones
(wearing thin silver spectacle rims)
to show Sam's mother how to relax.
Though she looked retiring and feeble,
in the library she would fix
his mother on a sheeted table.
Spring. And the shaken little cherry
tree at their fence was all ahop
in song, and bloom was customary,
a sneezy air over their back stoop
and terrace, like the dust of women.
After his mother, she took Sam.
She'd gather an engrossing group
of pictures from her wooden box,
and several human vertebrae,
and as he lay out supine, say:
"Think of your head as a balloon
or something light, as if the rest
of you is simply hanging down—
that's the relaxing way to walk,
for then we never pull back
the shoulders, or push out the chest."
She'd poke her fingers in each crack,
and slowly he became resigned
to thinking this was permanent
until his mother lost her mind
and had to leave—Miss Perkins went.
Unlike his mother, who returned.

STYX

Down at the west river, pieces of thought
washed up. Someone had stumbled from the park?
Unclear whose thoughts they were, or what
they said if put together. It grew dark
as doctors speculated on a blood-clot
and police began (down to the lowliest clerk)
to run their microfiche, but soon forgot
to wonder what had driven him berserk,
this man they couldn't find, only his thoughts.
Left on the riverbank are many sorrows,
but no one really knows what the currents do.
Here evergreen and willows thrive, the dawn whites
of flowers: River, where no one hears the minnows
applaud the mottled sunlight they swim through.

IDEAS AS THINGS

Memory

is like a messenger in a Greek play
reporting to the king—
except the messenger is held to say
forever the same thing.

Fame

is a little box on a high shelf
he cannot reach himself,
even on tiptoes.
And for all he knows
it's not worth reaching for.
Not anymore.

Fate

is an air we begin
to feel in the warm countries
more obviously than here:

as life went on before,
so will it go for those
to come, the yet unborn.

UNDRESSING THE SALAD

Some things are impossible,
or at least very difficult,
such as undressing a salad,
or unringing a bell
(as the lawyers say).
You stand convicted of
your salad days, my beauty.
Hmm... those salad days.
Apparently you got
a lot along the way,
like cherry tomatoes, romaine
lettuce, croutons, avocado,
radishes, peppers, cucumber chunks,
feta and garlic garnishes,
mangoes, tangerine slices,
artichoke hearts, apricots,
raisins, berries, grapes,
arugula, not to mention
nuts and celery stalks
and who would say what else
with rich or tangy juices
doused all over them.
Undressing you today
I'm disappointed in you—
or else simply jealous.
You ate more than I did.

THE FIELD

Winds blow still in the long grasses.
A trampled path reminds me where
Fred and I saw a spotted deer
at dusk—in childhood. Time passes.

AFTER LONG ILLNESS

> ...when evening comes
> like a butterfly through the window
> —Fernando Pessoa

I am stepping lightly since my illness
and recovering at home reading Pessoa.
Everyone is talking about him—how
he liked quiet. Walked from house to office.
Sat in cafés. Spoke to only a few.
Spun his whole life out or the bulk of it
in Lisbon doing nothing in particular
beyond the sad pages—25,000 pages!
Reading Pessoa now I need less sleep
and wake up early refreshed by his pessimism.
He has stolen many of my ideas—
me, the ex-kleptomaniac who when young
ambled down city subways looking for
anything left behind, like a handbag
of grocery coupons, homburg, pipe, tan gloves
on a bench folded, things I didn't need;
who in my uncle's toolshed found an old
herb-bottle of bright colored sand in layers
(what a pretty grinding whirr the top made),
now am given this idle sneak Pessoa.

R.I.P.

She drowned years later
in sinbad water

old man he died
of a late horse-ride

one left his soul
in a swimming hole

one lost his life
to a Spanish knife

some will devise
their own demise

and others age
from page to page

THE FATHER

Let me take you by the hand, old gentleman.
There may be a few stories we haven't told
each other and the hour is late now.
Both of us are growing old
(and you are a good deal older than I am).
There is no other way
to the shore than by the trees.
It is better than you think to be blind.
Teller of tales, of beautiful long stories,
where are you going, and how?
Something still is asking us to find
my soul again, we have so much to say.
Quieter quieter here, it is a land
of waters. Let me take you by the hand.

HOW JOE GOT ZEN

When Joe was little
he went to the movies, he
went to the movies.

More than candy or
popcorn or pop he loved the
dusty cone of light.

The ticket stub grew
ragged and soft and even
warm in his pocket.

When Joe was little
he liked Ida Lupino
and Barbara Stanwyck.

A happy, shabby
cinema it was, where Joe
went to the movies.

Say hi! to *Joe the
Magician* in a red cape
waving a black wand.

Cards, multicolored
handkerchiefs pulled from the sleeves,
silver rings, applause!

Ivory: he loved
his grandmother's dominoes
that went to 16.

High up he yelled down
her great circular staircase,
pretending to fall.

He became adult
and learned about Plato's cave
and the prisoners.

The prisoners, too,
saw images flickering
on a screen or wall.

So is there nothing
real, he began to wonder,
even the movies?

The movies, of course,
are real, although no more real
than anything else.

And why must life drift
away so quickly? Bring back
the old lamplighter,

the Hurdy-gurdy
man with his hatted monkey
rattling a tin cup.

When the sycamore
loses leaves to an autumn
wind, we know its shape.

On quiet eves he
hung around watching TV
documentaries.

The attack that brought
WWII
loomed up on the tube.

He joined the army
and fought when necessary,
yet it seemed senseless.

How had the whole globe
escaped annihilation,
himself included?

Could any man's life
escape annihilation,
his own included?

MBA in hand,
he joined a dull company
called Jefferson Soups.

Marrying, he had
two children, two healthy ones,
a boy and a girl.

Soon he came into
money and built a *pied-
à-terre* on the coast.

His tired dog grew
older and curled cozily
in his box all day.

Endless... the buzzing
crickets, an August whitethroat,
roll of the great sea.

Yet cities, nations
rise and fall, a craziness
people call progress.

To him the madness
of the world seemed absolute.
He became obsessed.

He bought a volume
on Japanese gardens, gray
stones in a raked garden.

Wherever you stood
a column would block one stone,
you never saw all.

Even these photos
could draw a person to the
mystery of Zen.

His small daughter grew
beautiful and smart, his son
said quick-witted things.

One day he saw that
life is forever only
what it is: one day.

His wife planted seeds
after a certain year, in
the dooryard crevice.

As luck would have it
a small rain fell at the right
time for the flowers.

He kissed his children,
deciding to take a short
walk before supper.

He sat on a rock
by the water a long time
for no good reason.

Sun behind hills dimmed....
Moon and pin-prick stars appeared....
And the new Joe laughed!

And that's the story
(although you didn't ask me)
of how Joe got Zen.

TROLLS

The old stones of Norway
craggy and rough and gray
(and colder in the darkness)
once were trolls, they say.

Trolls are selfish creatures
with twinkly, creepy features,
and many are alive.
They always will survive

even if tricked or fooled
as Ibsen knew so well.
Hooray for Ibsen-o
for he revealed it all:

He said the usual man
fights trolls in the outer world;
the artist or the great one
fights the trolls in his soul.

PROSPERO YOUNG AND OLD

I

All day the clouds blew east and the sun
let go the winter's cold
from grass under my running feet
where I lived in a competent world.

II

But often later
before opening
my eyes, I'd wonder
what bed I'm in,
what country or town,
alone or not—
in my daughter's home,
in my son's in Italy?
boats I've taken
if only to honor
the married, the dead;
by some middling field
lying on straw
disoriented,
or resting above
an English pub
as whoops of laughter
and tinkling glasses
rang into the night—
any of these?
or maybe instead
another bed.

III

How to grow old? to leave a shiny dot
of yourself somewhere. And what's the point?
This cloudy globe will go,
will disappear long after I grow faint.
And go by water, as Leonardo said,
not ice or fire, no waiting dead
awakened and whimpering,
no judgment day—but waves and crests
and currents sweeping off
the towers and pyramids and little homes
and everything man-made and more.

But as for now—how to grow old?
be rested, humorous,
nothing foretold.

WE THINK OF ARTHUR
TONÍ
DUANE

One by one the songs fade.
Here and there a word
is missing. Maybe I'd
pick up a line, or you'd
recall a chord
of what a mere decade
ago we sang and played.

SOLSTICE

Who is running around the tree this late summer evening?

They are not running, they are dancing.

Ah! Dancing, are they? Barefoot on grass and fern?

This particular day there is always leftover light.

So they are old spirits, but looking younger—right?

Yes, they are both young and old.

I see a ribbon floating from each to the tree,
But why do the ribbons not wind up, as on a maypole?

Perhaps the tree turns as they turn.

I hear a rustle of leaves, but can't see whole.
Tonight is summer solstice, and I fear the cold
And dark will come more readily and soon.
When the world's weight is on us, what will we do?

They are dancing. They have more faith than you.

JUMPING

My feet come down
on the holiday carpet

jumping—my rope goes
up and down,

up and down,
this early ritual

exercise.
I must suppose

We're more adroit
nowadays than when

under the sun
this way and that

we swung in the trees,
or earlier lay flat

on a rock to the moon,
all shadow and silhouette

turning a thin
profile

to the tideglaze—
where in the dross

of deep sea-glossaries
the tingling wan

fishes spun out
their destinies

going up and down.
O think of it,

the colors we've won
since we came in

touching the wheel!
And we were smart

to anticipate
the galaxies,

to be there in
the bursting grain

of love, or light,
or whatever it was,

hearing the night-
long whirl of cloven

stars, black holes, spinners
that flash and doze

in dots of braille
to uncurl

a universe
of stone afloat

like tapestries
unwinding. All

this wasn't news
to us, of course,

who had the beat
already, the will

to work and rise
(jump forty-nine!)

and socialize.
Sometimes I regret

my jumping chart,
it's hard to feel

at ease in a ripple
of entropies

running on down
the shadowcone

of years and years,
but any feat

is possible
if we retain

the leaf and tendril
sleeping in the brain,

the lost starfish, this cool
and perfect dawn

helping me get
my jumping done

and quick to praise
our holy season

among the sun
and other stars.

ACKNOWLEDGMENTS

Grateful acknowledgment is made to the editors of the magazines and presses in which the following poems first appeared:

American Weave (also reprinted in a pamphlet by the Academy of American Poets): "Croquet Lover at the Dinner Table"; *Beloit Poetry Journal:* "Loss of the Unicorn," "Walking Home" (originally "Young Shakeresses Walking Home"), "The Blot," *Wade's Wait* (chapbook 18); *The Chicago Review:* "Winter Fantasy"; *Inlet:* "Watchers" (originally "Fable"); *The Kentucky Poetry Review:* "Bread"; *Lucille:* "Country Matters," "Suite"; *The Massachusetts Review:* "To a Young Lady at the Museum"; Mitre Press (England): "Van Gogh: *Starry Night*"; Puckerbrush Press: the Michelangelo translations; *Puckerbrush Review:* "Generation," "Flacker in Paris," "After Long Illness"; *Quarry* (Canada): "The Snake" (originally "Genesis"), "The Millennial Laws," "Half-Song"; *Quartet:* "Homage to Shakers"; *Twigs:* "The Glassblower," "Bells"; *West Coast Poetry Review:* "At Home"; *Wisconsin Poetry Magazine:* "Willow Street."

I'm grateful to the editors at University of Missouri Press for *Croquet Lover at the Dinner Table,* and to Wolfe Editions, Limerock Books, and Bakery Studios, publishers of several of my previous books.

Published here for the first time are *Tivoli,* "Owed to *Finnegans Wake,*" and many poems in the last section.

"Traveling West" was first published in *American Weave* (1965-66) and was not originally in *Croquet Lover at the Dinner Table.*

For encouragement and advice over the years I want to give my warm thanks to Hugh Ector, Louis O. Coxe, Marion Stocking (all deceased); to my long-range writing group of Christopher Queally, Hugh Hennedy, Nancy Aldrich, Alicia Fisher, Keith Walker, Anne Dewees, and Joan Henson; and to David Riley, Megan Grumbling, Baird Whitlock, and Joseph Chaney, my chief editor at Indiana University South Bend.

JONATHAN ALDRICH was author of eight volumes of poetry. At Harvard College he won the Lloyd McKim Garrison Prize for poetry and the Academy of American Poets Prize. He was a Frost Scholar at The Bread Loaf School of English (from which he received his M.A. in 1964); Principal of Argenta Friends School in British Columbia, Canada; Assistant Director of The Bread Loaf Writers' Conference; and teacher of English at various colleges, including Berea College in Berea, Kentucky, and of English and Liberal Arts for twenty-five years at Maine College of Art, at which he was recognized for a "Best Teacher" award by faculty vote. His translation of Charles Baudelaire's "Le Voyage," illustrated by Alison Hildreth and hand-printed by David Wolfe Productions, won a Baxter Society Award. Aldrich was a trustee and volunteer for Portland Stage Company for twenty years. He and his wife, Nancy, have two grown married children, Tom (Carrie Nakamura) and Tess (Anthony Alessandrini), and two granddaughters, Junie Aldrich and Mina Alessandrini.

Poem titles are set in Trump Mediaeval LT Std.
Poem bodies are set in Garamond.

www.ingramcontent.com/pod-product-compliance
Lightning Source LLC
Chambersburg PA
CBHW080500240426
43673CB00006B/248